JUST
PLAY!

Vinita Sidhartha has a degree in journalism from the University of Texas at Austin, US. After completing her studies, she returned to India and set up a communications consultancy with leading clients from the corporate and media sectors.

As a mother of two, she turned to her grandmother to take care of her children. Her grandmother spent hours with the children teaching them a number of traditional Indian games. Watching this, the personal and the professional merged in Vinita. Thus, was born Kreeda, meaning play in Sanskrit, which researches and markets traditional games that are Indian in spirit and global in quality. (Visit www.kreedagames.com for more information.)

Vinita continues to use her communication skills to consult in the development sector. She is also the director at Power Centre Private Limited, an IT company, where she handles the marketing and HR functions.

Vinita loves writing about life, experiences and the memorable people she meets in life. Her blog is https://vinitasidhartha.in.

JUST PLAY!

Life Lessons from Traditional Indian Games

Vinita Sidhartha

RUPA

Published by
Rupa Publications India Pvt. Ltd 2022
7/16, Ansari Road, Daryaganj
New Delhi 110002

Sales centres:
Allahabad Bengaluru Chennai
Hyderabad Jaipur Kathmandu
Kolkata Mumbai

ISBN: 978-93-5520-569-8

First impression 2022

10 9 8 7 6 5 4 3 2 1

The moral right of the author has been asserted.

To my father,
I could have never done this without you.

CONTENTS

FOREWORD

For the past four decades or more, Indian games have been fading out of the market, leaving behind only the charming remnants found in rural fairs or haats. These are made of cheap wood and decorated with local paints, or made in tribal areas where most of the toys are made of terracotta. Being crudely made, it is impossible for them to attain the safety standards required for toys in the West.

We all have enjoyed the simple spinning tops, the rattles that had to be spun to make a loud clattering noise and the circular plate that had chickens pecking at imaginary grain when you gently rotated the round weight tied to a string that hung below. Some of these can still be found in the narrow lanes of crowded old bazaars; models of autorickshaws and motorcycles painted in bright colours are still exported. Rigid and lifeless dolls on most shelves of state emporia cannot compete with today's Barbie doll culture or video games that draw children into combating aggressively.

India is now undergoing a cultural reawakening, in which instead of cheap synthetic imports or imitations, we are looking into our own wellspring of knowledge. All outcomes of our creative work in the areas of traditional art, craft, textiles, architecture, and now games and toys, are returning to the origins of their meaning, purpose, history or the mythology that has sustained and enriched them. India's craft culture has always been rooted in a purpose that was either spiritual or utilitarian.

Vinita Sidhartha, the author of this fascinating and illuminating book, *Just Play!* has turned the searchlight to the deeper meaning of India's traditional games in areas where she has worked for many years. It combines historical research and presents us with a clear vision of what is now called 'social design'. She shares with us how each game has relevance for the individual, the local and the global community, teaching us about ethics and values. The earliest learnings are presented in this labour of love through the important teachings of our culture and civilization. It is a true delight to share such a valuable exploration.

Jaya Jaitly
Activist, Author and Promoter of Handicrafts
17 April 2022

AUTHOR'S NOTE

When I started researching these games, they were mere games to me. But the more I read about them and played them, the more I realized that there were many messages and lessons hidden within them. Were they designed with these in mind? We will probably never know.

As far as the games in this book are concerned, I have tried to focus on their different aspects—aspects that interested me and have some impact on our lives.

Understanding these games took me on a journey of learning more about Indian philosophy, sociology, psychology and human life itself. I am not an expert, but an explorer, and what I have learnt has fascinated me, and this is what I have tried to share with you through this book.

This book is by no means exhaustive. It is my journey to understand the games and through them the charm and wealth of Indian culture, and how it could perhaps influence our lives. If I have made mistakes or left out anything, forgive me, for I am still learning and there is much that I have to learn.

There is a tendency in all of us, to look for answers to life in religion, philosophy, faith and beyond. But perhaps, maybe just perhaps, some of these answers can be found in our simple traditional games.

If this is so, losing these games would be a tragedy. If you find this book enjoyable, it is the games that have made it so. Therefore, I ask you, each and every one of you, to do your bit in reviving these games and keeping them alive for future generations.

If in any way, I can assist you in this endeavour, or if you would like to know more about these games or share with me the ones you are aware of that might disappear into oblivion, please do contact me at vinnisidh@gmail.com.

AN INTRODUCTION TO TRADITIONAL GAMES OF INDIA

Walk into a store, any store, and you come across an array of brightly packaged games for all ages and tastes. As you scan the shelves, you see games that reflect the life of the twentieth and twenty-first centuries—The Game of Life, Monopoly, Risk, Scotland Yard and many more.

And somewhere tucked away, you will stumble upon some old favourites from childhood—Ludo, and Snakes and Ladders. Perhaps they will bring a smile to your face as you remember a long-forgotten memory. Perhaps you will remember a friend, a neighbour or a cousin and how you laughed together over a game.

But when you are confronted by somebody talking about traditional games of India steeped in the culture of the land, you are left puzzled. You shake your head because you have no idea about the games they are talking about. And therein lies the tragedy, for the games of Ludo, and Snakes and Ladders, which are perhaps the most popular of childhood games across the world, have their origins in India.

All About Snakes and Ladders

Generations of children have experienced the thrill of climbing a ladder and the despair of landing on a snake, plunging them to the bottom of the board. What most people do not know is that this seemingly simplistic children's game is a complex one that originated in India. The game, in essence, deals with spirituality, morality and the journey of the soul. With names such as *Parama Padam Sopanam* (Steps to the Highest Place), *Moksha Patam* (The Path to Moksha or Liberation), *Gyan Path* (The Path to Knowledge) or *Vaikunta Pali* (The Route to Heaven), the purpose of the game is crystal clear.

Little is known about who created this game. Popular opinion attributes it to Gnyanadev, a thirteenth-century saint, who was part of the Bhakti movement. Another theory attributes it to the Jains—a pictorial effort to spread Jain philosophy and the theory of karma.

No matter who created the game, it grew in popularity. The traditional boards were diverse, with differing numbers of squares and a varied placement of snakes and ladders. But one aspect was standard across all boards: every snake represented a vice and every ladder a virtue. Boards were peppered with illustrations representing the journey through life. As many of these were printed on paper, they have disappeared into oblivion. Luckily, a few survive to tell us this remarkable story.

Today, it is primarily regarded as a Vaishnava game, played on the night of the festival of Vaikunta Ekadashi—the eleventh day in the ninth month of the lunar calendar. On that day, a special door in the temples is opened, which is symbolic of a direct route to heaven. People stay up all night, fasting and praying, and playing the game to pass the time.

Today, the game has lost its moral overtones, and people all over the world play it with little understanding of its significance. The game represents a person's journey through life, overcoming vices and acquiring virtues in a struggle to become a better human being, an evolved soul and reach *parama padam* or the highest place.

A traditional board with notations for virtues and vices
Photo credit: Author's collection

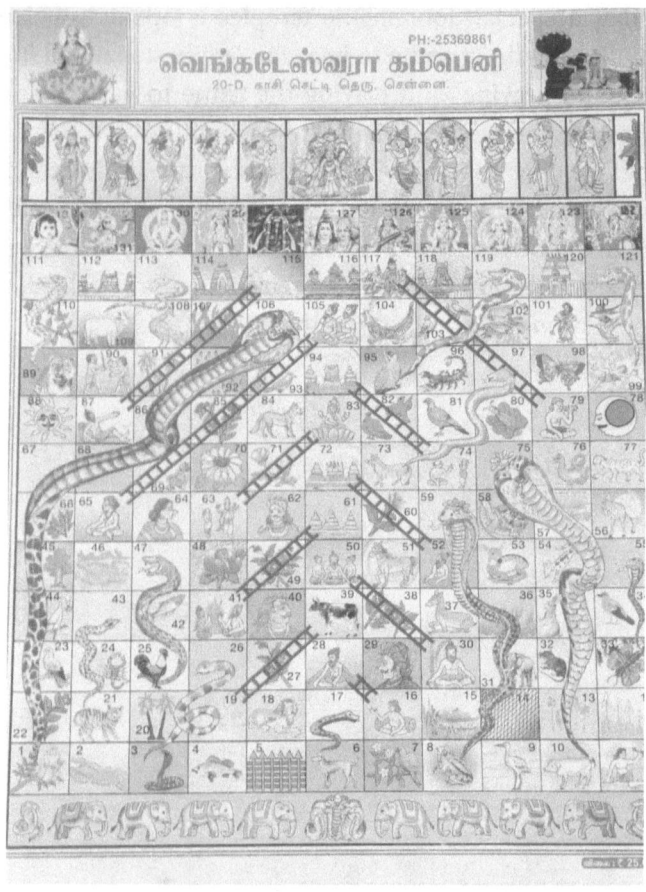

A more modern board of the game with no notations
Photo credit: Author's collection

A modern Snakes and Ladders with no sign of the
traditional elements—Pattachitra from Orissa
Photo credit: Author's collection

Chaupad: The Game That Became Ludo

The game of Ludo, on the other hand, has its roots in Chaupad, which is perhaps the most widespread and best known of the traditional games of India even today. It is sometimes referred to as the national game. It is played on a board shaped like a symmetrical cross. From the number of squares on each arm, the presence of corner squares, to the use of dice or cowries as throw pieces, the rules are all defined by the regional variations of the game.

Legend has it that this is the game referred to in the Mahabharata. In fact, keeping in mind the ensuing quarrel between the cousins, in the epic, some believe that the first throw of the dice should never be played. That throw is nullified with a prayer that the game not lead to disputes among the players.

According to another legend, this is the game of dice that was played by Shiva and Parvati. A poem talks about the game played by the young couple, where the desire to win competes with the desire for an embrace or kiss, which is the penalty for a loss.

> An embrace at first
> And then a loving kiss had been her losses in the gambling match.
> Now when her lover asks again for stakes,
> She is silent, though the flush upon her cheek
> rises with suppressed excitement,
> And her hand is sweating as she moves the piece.
>
> (*Subhasitaratnakosa*, 605, attributed to Rajasekhara)

Some even believe that it is this game that is referred to in the poem 'The Gambler's Lament' in the Rig Veda:

> Play no longer with the dice, but till your field
> Enjoy what you possess, and value it highly
> There are your cattle, and there is your wife,
> O gambler.

A game of Chaupad in progress on the sidewalks of Ajmer
Photo credit: Author

History tells us that Emperor Akbar played the game on a giant board of marble in Fatehpur Sikri. One can almost picture the scene—a moonlit night with oil lamps punctuating the darkness and incense sticks wafting delicate tendrils of sandalwood and jasmine, while women from his harem, wearing colour-coordinated clothes to represent the game pieces, flit about on the board, accompanied by the soft jingle of their anklets at the throw of the imperial dice. History and legend aside, it is a game that continues to fascinate people through the years.

In contrast to the game of Parama Padam Sopanam, which has a more spiritual origin, the game of Chaupad is often dismissed as frivolous and simplistic. However, the interplay of choice and chance—with the dice providing the element of chance and the decision on moves providing the choice—makes the game, perhaps, the best representation of real life and the challenges we face.

Why Traditional Games?

While Chaupad and Parama Padam have found a new lease of life through the games of Ludo, and Snakes and Ladders, respectively, and continue enjoying popularity, albeit in a more simplistic form, other games from India have not been so fortunate.

Some continue to reside in the memories of the older generation, while others have disappeared into the cobwebs of their minds. This is particularly true of the vast variety of games played with seeds, stones, shells and twigs, for our ancestors did not buy games from shops. They literally plucked them from trees and picked them up from the ground. Materials available around them were transformed into exciting games. Once the games were over, the items were tossed away, left to become one with the earth. With no written rules or permanent play pieces, nothing survives of these games but memories.

Board games have been a little more fortunate. Many of them have been inscribed on stone floors of temples, monuments and homes, where they remain a silent reminder of a time gone by, when these games provided leisure, entertainment, camaraderie and an insight into human life. Game pieces excavated from archaeological sites tell us that even a thousand years ago, people used to play just like we do today.

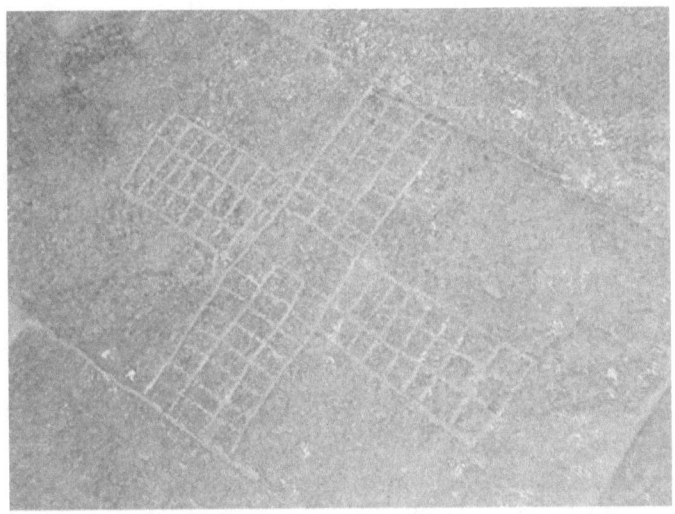

An etching of Dayakattam or Chaupad at the
Dhenupureeswarar Temple, Madambakkam, Chennai
Photo credit: Kreeda

Dr Venkatarama Raghavan, the author of *Festivals, Sports and Pastimes of India*, says many of the festivals would have religion as one aspect, with enjoyment, music, dance and games forming essential parts of the celebrations. The festivals were rooted in the 'phenomena of Nature, of earth and sky, of the sun and the moon, of vegetation, trees, flowers and fruits, of the changing face and attractions of Nature which the march of seasons provided.'[1]

Traditional games across the world have deep roots in the culture, beliefs, environment and customs of the society

---

[1]Raghavan, Dr Venkatarama, *Festivals, Sports and Pastimes of India*, B. J. Institute of Learning and Research, 1979, p. 13.

in which they are born. The impact of the environment on games is more commonly observed in those played with seeds and fruits. The popularity of tamarind in South Indian cooking has engendered a whole range of games played with tamarind seeds. The popularity of the coconut tree and its copious use in Indian cuisine led to the creative use of the shells in Coconut Shell Walk.

From Tamarind Seeds to Fun Games

A popular element in traditional games is the tamarind seed. The word 'tamarind' is believed to be derived from the Persian Tamar-i-Hind or Indian date.[2] It is a pod-like fruit, which, on turning ripe, produces a brown, edible pulp used in cuisines around the world. The pulp is also used in traditional medicine and as a metal polish. The tree can be used for woodworking and the tender young leaves are used in cooking. As tamarind has multiple uses, it is cultivated around the world in tropical and subtropical zones. Particularly in South India, nearly every house had a tamarind tree as the pulp was used in everyday cooking. The seeds, meanwhile, made for wonderful play material. The semi-rectangular smooth seeds were used as game pieces or counters. Seeds cut in half were often used as throw pieces in place of cowrie shells.

---

[2]Bhadoriya, Santosh Singh et. al., 'Tamarindus indica: Extent of explored potential', *Pharmacognosy Review*, Vol. 5, No. 9, January–June 2011, pp. 73–81, https://bit.ly/3sY2Hpu. Accessed on 4 April 2022.

Tamarind seeds cut in half and used as dice
Photo credit: Kreeda

Whole seeds were used in games that involved blowing on them such that they were scattered. It was then followed by picking them up one by one, without touching another. This seemingly simple game tested not just the lung capacity of the player but also their fine motor skills.

*A game with tamarind seeds—picking one
by one without moving the others
Photo credit: Kreeda*

Sadly, with space constraints and the slow but obvious transition to apartments, the backyard tree started becoming a thing of the past. Packaged and cleaned tamarind sold in shops is the new norm, so most children do not even know that tamarind comes from trees. They do not know that if one has a collection of these seeds—well-aired and stored—it can provide hours of fun.

It is believed that all trees are created from the hair of Brahma, the lord of creation. Tamarind trees, which are already interwoven with our lives and culture, make for a truly divine creation.

The Coconut Shell Walk

With its markings, which look like three eyes, and the tuft at the top, a coconut almost looks like a human head. Hence, breaking a coconut is believed to be akin to breaking or surrendering the ego. Another belief is that since the coconut provides people with all that is essential for life, the act of breaking it is symbolic of surrendering everything. The custom of presenting a coconut to an honoured guest is seen as a symbol of giving or sharing with them all that is yours.

The tree is believed to be of great value in the tropical regions because it provides all the essential elements needed to sustain life there. Besides serving as a good source of food and drink, it offers raw materials for housing, thatching, clothing, containers, oil, brooms, ornaments, furniture, and of course, toys and games.

Ready for the Coconut Shell Walk: Coconut shells with tied rope
Photo credit: Kreeda

Coconut Shell Walk is a folk game found in countries of Southeast Asia as well as the Pacific islands. It is played using two halved coconut shells to which a rope is attached. The player walks on the shells, holding the rope between the first two toes, while pulling on it with the hands to keep balance and help lift the shells while walking.

Dr Andrew Topsfield, who was the curator of the Ashmolean Museum of Art and Archaeology in Oxford and one of the authorities on the game of Snakes and Ladders, says, 'Play is a basic element of human life and playing of games is found in virtually every society in the world... Games which in themselves might appear culturally neutral...could become endowed with complex overlays...or symbolic meanings.'[3]

These basic and elemental human impulses are common to people across the world. And it is this human impulse, this creative response, that leads to the development of games—a miniature imitation of the world we live in.

Dr Irving Finkel, one of the world's leading authorities on traditional games, says, 'While early games mirrored the simpler nomadic lifestyle of early humans, as societies evolved and became more complex, so did the games. It is evident that their appearance on the stage of human social evolution coincides with the development of structured and sedentary communal living associated with shared

[3]Topsfield, Andrew, *The Art of Play: Board and Card Games of India*, The Marg Foundation, Mumbai, 2007, pp. 12–13.

responsibility and labour. It is under these circumstances that leisure first makes itself apparent and it is surely leisure that is the prime requirement for the invention and play of board games.'[4]

It is understandable that board games have become increasingly complex over time. But this does not change the fact that they still mirror basic human impulses and aspirations, such as the desire for companionship, the desire to succeed, the desire to triumph over evil or obstacles and the desire for harmony.

The elemental appeal of traditional games sets them apart from the games of today, as they transcend social, cultural, educational and linguistic barriers. That accounts for its strength and relevance in the twenty-first century. Life, society and culture might have changed, but basic human aspirations stay the same.

The Need to Play

'I remember that sixty-seventy years ago much of the recreation and fun was within large undivided families. Dayakattam (Chaupad) was one of the popular games of those times. The *kattam* (grid) was drawn on the ground. Competition was fierce and noisy. Participation cut across generations and sometimes even the neighbours would join in. There would also be active spectators, encouraging one side or the other. Over weekends, this would go on

---

[4]Finkel, Irving (ed), *Ancient Board Games in Perspective*, British Museum Press, London, 2007, p. 1.

to become a long session extending to a good four to five hours.'

These words from an elderly lady, well into her eighties, conjure up images of large and boisterous family gatherings on lazy unstructured weekends with the entire family coming together—grey-haired grandparents, authoritative uncles, bustling aunts and a brood of children. Surely the game would be accompanied by copious amounts of hot coffee carefully poured into gleaming steel tumblers with just the right amount of froth, the steam rising lazily and the aroma wafting all around. Perhaps, there would be a mound of gleaming, golden, brown and crisp bhajjis or fritters with translucent onions or with slices of melting soft potatoes. Accompanied by raised voices, laughter and mock fights that are all part of such a game would be the ringing sound of the long brass dice rolling on the floor. It was not just the game but the entire spirit of tradition and of families and people coming together in a shared experience that would create memories lasting a lifetime.

Sadly, days like those are slowly but surely disappearing from our lives. With the breakdown of the traditional joint family system, the advent of television, rising media penetration and technology bringing the wonder of the entire world into our homes, our ideas of leisure and pastime have changed. More families with working parents and increased workloads have resulted in adults finding little or no time to indulge in such games.

A multi-generational game session in progress
Photo credit: Kreeda

In the case of children, the pressure to succeed, do better than their peers and get ahead of the curve has resulted in spontaneous games becoming an increasingly rare occurrence. To quote a teacher: 'There are no backyards anymore, or large verandas...and the children go from the confinement of the classroom to the confinement of the tuition room, or are bundled off to practise for some competitive sport.'

But play is an impulse native to man. Dr Raghavan, in his book, says play is not a luxury, nor is it something frivolous. It is the very core of our being. He says the idea of play is 'one of the bases of civilization.' He adds, 'The spirit of playful competition is, as a social impulse, older than culture itself and pervades all the life like a veritable ferment.'

This is also reflected in the book *Homo Ludens: A Study of the Play-Element in Culture* by the Dutch historian and cultural theorist Johan Huizinga, who suggests that play is primary to and a necessary condition for the generation of culture. Huizinga begins by making it clear that animals played before humans. He says, 'Play is older than culture, for culture, however inadequately defined, always presupposes human society, and animals have not waited for man to teach them their playing.'[5]

This interplay between games and life, where each draws inspiration from and mirrors the other, is an important element in understanding human thinking and, therefore, the importance of understanding and reviving our traditional games.

From games carved on the floors of temples and monuments, to memories of play that linger in the minds of people, from art, literature and sculpture, we discover our rich history and culture of traditional games. We need to bridge the gap between the past and the present to identify the relevance of the games today without disturbing their intrinsic form, beauty and essence.

In 1793, Harikrishna, author of *Kreedakausalyam*, described the famous games of his time: 'I hereby describe the organisation, structure, and rules of this ancient shastra, the reason being that...scholars do not study them. In this book there is a description of several board games; the intention of this shastra being that

---

[5]Huizinga, Johan, *Homo Ludens: A Study of the Play-Element in Culture*, Beacon Press, 1971, p. 1.

people will enhance their brain power by studying them.'[6]

He believed that games were a shastra (science) from which we could learn a lot. Over 200 years later, although a few individuals and organizations are working on the revival of traditional games, the fact remains that the time for games and play is slowly disappearing from our lives.

What perhaps is required is to capture the essence of traditional games while merging it with the practical demands of the day. Today, in the harum-scarum world of the twenty-first century, we need these games. We need them to create a magic circle, as known in digital games—a space in which the normal rules and the reality of the world are suspended and replaced by the artificial reality that the game offers. It is here that we find the space to build relationships, forget the cares of the real world and discover ourselves.

Building Relationships Through Games

In a world gone crazy, where time is of essence, the closest of relationships break. Perhaps, one of the greatest challenges we face today is building relationships that stand the test of time. Here, play offers a distinct advantage. When two people play together, each influences the other's experience. The experience and enjoyment in play varies with different people—be it a significant other, a child, a parent, a friend or a colleague. This is distinct from watching, say television together, where the enjoyment often depends on the content

---

[6]Harikrishna, *Kreedakausalyam*, Nag Publishers, New Delhi, 1982.

rather than the people you are watching with. This makes play a shared experience rather than merely a common one.

Bryan Jeffrey, an American businessman, whose expertise is in marketing with a focus on communication, says, 'Shared experiences are powerful because they bring people together and have a deep impact on human socialization because they enhance each person's individual experience.'[7]

Swami Vivekananda had said the same thing when he differentiated between contact and connection. He said, 'Connection is between heart and heart... Sitting together, sharing meals and caring for each other, touching, shaking hands, having eye contact, spending some time together... in short, shared experiences.'[8]

Playing traditional games together is a powerful shared experience that helps build relationships that could last a lifetime. Everyone has a memory from their childhood—of a happy summer day filled with laughter, playing games with a friend. It does not matter where you go or what you do, when you meet that friend again, you are transported back to that memorable experience you shared. Nothing and no one can ever take that away from you. You and your friend will forever share that special experience.

[7]Kramer, Bryan Jeffrey, *Shareology: How Sharing Is Powering the Human Economy*, Morgan James Publishing, New York, 2015.
[8]Burke, Mary Louise, *Swami Vivekananda in the West: New Discoveries*, Advaita Ashrama; 4th edition, 1957.

Managing Stress

Happy thoughts, laughter and memories are balm to the mind and soul. In 1266, King Alfonso X of Castile, in his *Book of Games* said that God wanted man to have all kinds of happiness in himself naturally, so that he could face the cares and troubles when they came his way. Men sought many ways to achieve this happiness completely. So they found and developed many types of play and pieces to delight themselves with.

Games provide a momentary pause in life, allowing us to have a bit of fun. In today's stressed environment, these pauses, along with the fun, laughter and companionship that naturally come along, become critical in managing stress. Some traditional games may have been designed to have a better and more direct impact on battling stress. The game of *Pallanguzhi* involves the repetitive handling of small objects with one's fingers. This tactile and repetitive action is akin to playing with Kombolói, also known as worry beads. This is a string of beads similar to prayer beads and native to the Greek and Cypriot culture. They help calm one's mind. Modern variations of worry beads include the stress ball and the fidget spinner.

Pallanguzhi: A Game and Stress Buster

Pallanguzhi is a fascinating game of distribution. It is known by several names across India and the world.

This game has been traditionally played using seeds, shells or stones on a series of depressions made on the ground by the heel of the palm. However, wooden boards of great intricacy and workmanship are also found.

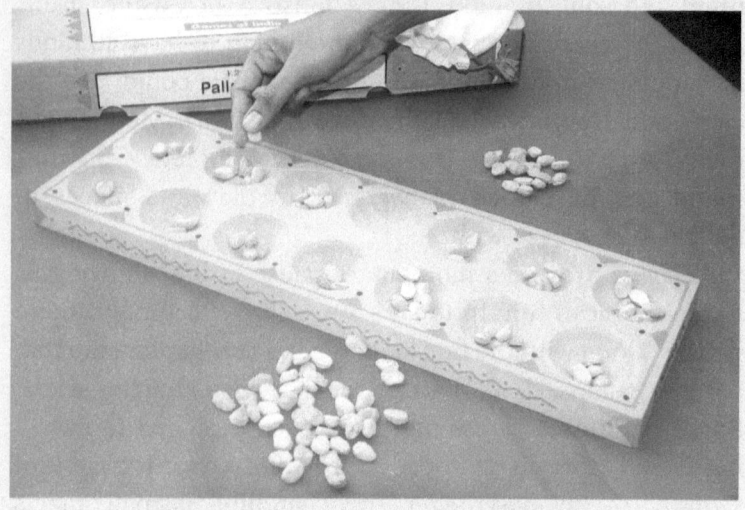

Dropping counters on a Pallanguzhi board
Photo credit: Kreeda

The essence of the game stays the same in all variations—the players drop the game pieces in the pits and collect treasure based on the outcome of that distribution. The game is played by picking up the pieces in your hand and deftly dropping them with your fingers. The movement of the fingers is similar to manipulating prayer beads.

The Emotional Mental Imagery Lab (EMIL) for psychological treatment development run by Emily Holmes conducted a study on the impact of similar mechanisms in managing stress.[9] The study volunteers watched graphic footage of car wrecks. Over the next week, images of the victims occasionally came back to haunt them. It was found that people who typed a simple, repetitive pattern on a keyboard while they watched the film suffered fewer flashbacks. According to their theory, that's because keeping your hands busy could reduce stress.

The Purpose of This Book

The last 20 years spent on researching and understanding traditional games has led me to a whole new understanding of myself, the culture of India and basic human impulses. As we play, we disappear into the suspended reality of a game, and it is in this space that we often find our true selves. Every game represents or captures an aspect of life and the world we live in. But unlike life, games can be played again and again, getting it right. Making mistakes in the real world has lasting impact. Making mistakes in a game has limited consequences. It is through mistakes that we learn and grow. This aspect of games allows us to understand various aspects of our personality and abilities, such as the practical, the tactical, the attitudinal and the strategic.

Neil Gaiman, the well-known author, remarks: 'If you are making mistakes, then you are making new things, trying new things, learning, living, pushing yourself, changing the world. You're doing things you've never done

---

[9]Holmes, E.A. et al., 'Trauma Films, Information Processing, and Intrusive Memory Development', *Journal of Experimental Psychology*, Vol. 133, Issue 1, 2004, https://bit.ly/3MzB0ve. Accessed on 4 April 2022.

before, and more importantly, you're doing something.'[10]

The board used in games simulates real life and gives the player a chance to rehearse thinking and experimenting in a stress-free environment without the fear of repercussions and consequences.

While initially I was happy to just research the games and rules of play, I became more interested in their relevance in the twenty-first century. Do old games have a place in this technology-driven world? With their languid pace, are they relevant in the real-time fast-paced world we live in? The more I thought about it, the more people I interacted with—from senior management professionals to trainers, mentors, life coaches and common people—the more convinced I was of the importance of these games.

Creative Problem-Solving

These games reduce life's complexity to a replica of elements. They lessen the pressure of the environment, enabling the player to view complexity in a calm and objective manner, and helping them isolate the core of the problem. Unlike in real life, one move or another in a game does not result in shattering consequences. The move that was not taken up can be tried the next time to test its consequences—this is often not plausible in real life. Thus, playing games enables us to expose ourselves to outcomes of different patterns

---

[10]Gaiman, Neil, 'I hope that in this year to come, you make mistakes....' *Lessons Learned in Life*, 30 December 2013, https://bit.ly/3DHwZ4B. Accessed on 5 April 2022.

of thinking and action. It encourages creativity in strategic and tactical approaches to handling difficult situations. It enables experimentation with out-of-the-box solutions, free from the fear of consequences.

The causal relationship between action and outcome in games is instant and repeatable with endless variations creating a variety of experiences. Participants—partners or opponents—as well as spectators can evaluate the personal qualities that each of them brings to problem-solving, and train themselves to apply those attitudes and abilities in real life.

Awareness and Openness

What is required today is a degree of self-awareness, consciously knowing and understanding one's own character, feelings, motives and desires. With self-awareness comes the ability to clinically assess oneself, to understand how we respond to situations and how we need to change.

An important advantage that comes with board games is the strong emotional involvement of the participants. The cognitive challenges, the excitement of the competition, the desire to excel and the hands-on approach—all contribute to greater awareness and openness to change as opposed to a conventional learning process.

In Conclusion

The games that have been discussed in this book are carefully selected on the basis of their popularity, appeal and the philosophy that defines them. You might feel daunted because you may either not recognize the games or the names that go with them. But do not worry—every chapter tells you about the game, its history and how to play it. Soon, you will find yourself at ease with each game, as they are rooted in our culture and somehow familiar to you.

All of these can be played on various levels—be it just for passing time, be it for social interaction with friends and family, or for self-analysis and growth. All we need to do is open up our minds, becoming conscious of ourselves, the game, its objectives and how we tackle the situations in game play.

As Plato is believed to have said, 'You can discover more about a person in an hour of play than in a year of conversation.' Through this book and the magic of traditional games, I hope to take you with me on a journey of discovery—a discovery of who you are, what you need and where you want to go. All you need to do is, *Just Play!*

Section 1

....

UNDERSTANDING THE SELF

'The only person you are destined to
become is the person you decide to be.'

—Ralph Waldo Emerson,
American author and philosopher

❖

*We are born with a certain genetic make-up and
biological traits. However, who we are as human
beings develops through social interaction. George
Herbert Mead, the American philosopher, sociologist
and psychologist, studied the self, the distinct identity
a person develops through social interaction.*

*He says, 'If a person wants to engage in the process
of "self", he/she must develop himself or herself through
the eyes of others. That's not an ability that we are
born with. Through socialization we learn to put
ourselves in someone else's shoes and look at the
world through their perspective. This assists us in*

becoming self-aware, as we look at ourselves from the perspective of the 'other.'[1]

Any effort at self-development requires introspection—an effort to examine oneself, rethink and change. The tools to do this are not scientific experiments, but simple everyday activities like a game. Panch Kone, a solitaire game, challenges you to try again and again to solve the puzzle, seek patterns and explore possibilities, and through this process understand yourself and how you relate to the world around you.

---

[1]"Theories of Self-Development', *Lumen*, https://bit.ly/3jBHzAQ. Accessed on 18 April 2022.

1

PANCH KONE[2]: CONTINUOUSLY CHALLENGING YOURSELF

The game of Panch Kone
Photo credit: Kreeda

---

[2]Also known as *Nakshatra Vilayattu, Nav Goti,* etc.

Every game we play is the result of a creative journey and a response to the environment. Whether it is the game of Monopoly—created in the early part of the twentieth century to reflect the buying, selling and development of land, which was critical to the economic mood of the time—or a fantasy online game today that takes you away from the stresses of everyday life, every game is a response to the environment and draws inspiration from it.

Traditional games, being more elemental, draw from simple symbols, everyday materials and the philosophies of our culture for inspiration. Some of these are echoed by people across the world. To take an example, a child hopping on a black-and-white chequered floor by jumping from one square to the other is responding creatively to the physical pattern implicit on the floor. A child anywhere in the world, if left to play in a room with such a floor, will instinctively respond to the pattern by creating games around it.

This is perhaps one explanation for how similar traditional games are found in different parts of the world. This also, perhaps, explains why the framework or grid of numerous traditional game boards echo patterns and symbols that are native to our culture or the elements found in the environment.

One of the most easily identifiable symbols is the five-pointed star, created by an unbroken line criss-crossing to form five points. Perhaps, every one one of us has scribbled these five-pointed stars in our schoolbooks with the unbridled glee that it could be drawn without lifting our pencil from the page.

Commonly, one point of the star points upwards, while two go left and right, and the other two point downwards. For those of us who have read *The Da Vinci Code* by Dan Brown and followed the adventures with bated breath, the meaning of symbols and the secrets hidden within them are greatly fascinating. This star provides all the fascination you need as it is replete with meaning and symbolism in almost all cultures across the world.

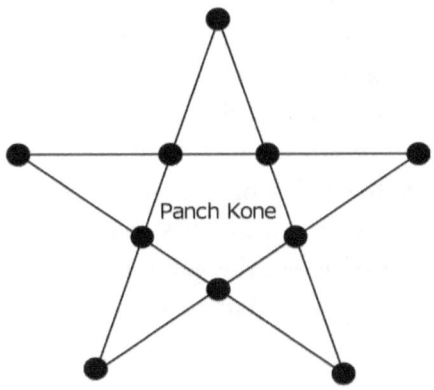

Illustration of the game of Panch Kone
Illustration credit: Kreeda

For Christians, it is often a symbol of the five wounds of Christ; to Muslims, the five pillars of their religion; to some, it represents the five senses and to others, the five elements of earth, wind, fire, water and ether. But beyond all else, to all of mankind, from time immemorial, the stars have awed us, fascinated us and have inspired us to dream.

Humans have long been fascinated by the stars—those tiny pinpoints of light that are scattered across the night sky and carry secrets of lands and worlds far, far away. No surprise that the star has grown to represent achievement—from the little schoolgirl whose teacher draws a star next to a perfect score on a test, to a greater number of stars symbolizing new heights of achievement or excellence, such as that of a five-star hotel. This symbol of accomplishment, which inspires us to reach beyond ourselves and venture into the unknown, resonates deeply with the human desire for success. And the game that captures this desire to improve, to learn, to challenge oneself continuously and grow is none other than the game of *Panch Kone*, the star game.

In many ways, unlike other games, the lessons in the game of Panch Kone are embedded in the very design of the board and the rules of the game. While the moves and strategies teach us numerous things, we need to first understand the essence of the game board and the rules to appreciate the lessons contained in them.

The Five-Pointed Star

The five-pointed star is made up of 10 points (the five points of the star and the five vertices of the inner pentagon) and 15 line segments. This forms the game board on which we play. This is a single-player game, a puzzle that we must solve. There are numerous single-player games in the world—board games, card games, puzzles, video games—each with its own rules, goals and challenges.

The first version of the game of Panch Kone is very similar to the popular Indian game of Brainvita. Nine game pieces are placed on nine of the 10 points on the board. One point is left empty. The focus of the game is on removing one game piece at a time by jumping over it to an empty space on the same straight line until there is only one game piece on the board. Although Brainvita is played on a different board with more game pieces, the concept remains the same.

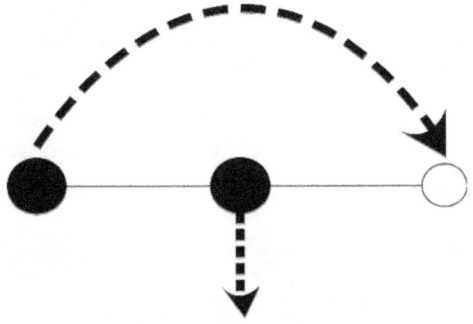

Game piece to be removed

Illustration showing the removal of game pieces
Illustration credit: Kreeda

Brainvita is the common name in India for Peg Solitaire or Solo Noble. The first version of the game can be traced back to the court of Louis XIV. There was even an engraving made of Anne de Rohan-Chabot, Princess of Soubise, with the puzzle by her side. In the August 1697 edition of the French literary magazine *Mercure Galant*, a description of the board, rules and sample problems were given.[3] This is the first-known reference to the game in print.

While the game of Peg Solitaire is known in the West, the version of the game played on the five-pointed star

---

[3]*Mercure Galant*, August 1697, p. 88

seems unique to India. Evidence of this game being played is mentioned in books and in interactions with local people from states as diverse as Rajasthan and Tamil Nadu.

In the city of Chennai in Tamil Nadu, evidence of this game can be found engraved on the floor of a number of temples. While it is easy to dismiss the pattern as just a star and not a board game, in one temple, the star is found engraved right next to and in the same format as another popular board game. This seems to validate the fact that it is perhaps indeed a board game, probably etched by craftsmen on the hard granite floors to pass their time.

Game boards inscribed on the floor of the
Kundrathur Murugan Temple, Chennai
Photo credit: Kreeda

How Do You Play?

With nine game pieces, play seems fairly easy at first, but an interesting twist comes while ensuring that one specific game piece, marked in some distinct manner, remains at the end, on a specific point on the board. This twist adds to the challenge in the game and further deepens the need for strategic thinking and planning.

The second version of the game is far more complex. It involves placing nine game pieces on nine points on the board following the strict rules of placement.

1. You count three points on the board in a straight line and place your game piece on the third point.
2. Your starting point must be empty.

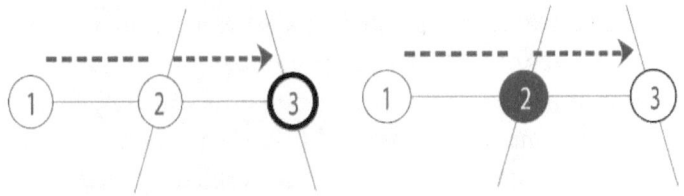

Illustration showing the rules of placement of game pieces
Illustration credit: Kreeda

Both versions of the game pose endless challenges. 'How many game pieces can I place or how many can I remove?' It requires thinking and strategy, and constantly refining your approach till you have only one game piece on the board in the first version or all nine on the board in the second. Some solitaire games, like the popular ones with playing cards are about chance and observation. This game is about refining your thinking process to play better and better with each effort.

Self-Growth and Learning from Mistakes

Single-player games offer numerous benefits that other games do not. In a world where we are constantly interacting with people, it offers a chance to enjoy one's own company, while challenging the mind and staying engaged. The absence of the stress of interaction with others soothes the mind and so does the repetitive nature of the moves that the game requires.

In addition, playing a solo repetitive game teaches us tremendous life lessons. Playing alone in a vacuum, with no other player to influence the game, the decisions, the moves, the results are ours and ours alone. In a world where the advice and actions of people around us often influence our thinking, it is easy to blame the outcome on such elements that are beyond our control. But this single-player game forces us to take ownership of the results, as all elements are within our control here. And if the results are not up to our expectations, we can play the game again and again honing our thinking, refining our strategy and perfecting the results. This constant effort to challenge ourselves to grow is not only important in this game but also for surviving in today's world.

Every game gives us a chance to suspend the reality of the world and provides us the opportunity to experiment with numerous approaches, perspectives and moves. Mistakes can be made and from these mistakes we learn and grow. Making a mistake in games may not be the end of the world, but in life we often pay dearly for them. Thus, games offer a respite from the brutality of the real world.

The decision made by the American soft drink giant Coca-Cola is a lesson in strategic thinking. The company had a classic, timeless flavour that was popular with all who favoured the brand. In 1985, in an attempt to compete with Pepsi, Coca-Cola came up with 'New Coke', a soda that tasted sweeter. The consumers were immensely disappointed and the flavour was considered a major failure.[4] The colossal failure of New Coke is a cautionary tale against tampering with a well-established and successful brand, and the price Coco-Cola paid for their mistake was tremendous.

Closer to home, we have another example: Prithviraj Chauhan was the ruler of Delhi and Ajmer when Muhammad Ghori was marching towards Delhi after conquering several parts of Punjab. Prithviraj was able to unite a few Rajput states to present a united front against the common enemy. Ghori was wounded and defeated. He was carried away from the battlefield by a soldier, and his army fled. The Rajputs did not follow the fleeing enemy—a blunder which cost them dearly, for Ghori returned the next year and defeated Prithviraj.

In contrast to the above instances, the game of Panch Kone offers a safe space to make mistakes and hone critical thinking abilities without the far-reaching consequences of

---

[4]Haoes, Rachid, '30 years ago today, Coca-Cola made its worst mistake', *CBS News*, 23 April 2015, https://cbsn.ws/3HaaTba. Accessed on 18 April 2022.

real-life scenarios. The game offers a space to challenge yourself and gradually improve till you reach perfection, or in this case, a successful conclusion to the game. Personal growth and perseverance are critical in the journey to all human achievements. Ralph Waldo Emerson, the popular American writer, once remarked, 'Unless you try to do something beyond what you have already mastered, you will never grow.' And growth is the true mantra for success. In the course of our lives, our environment is constantly evolving. For an individual or organization to succeed in this scenario, it would require one to constantly challenge and reinvent oneself.

Reinvent for Self-growth

The Covid-19 pandemic in 2020 was a prime example of the need to reinvent oneself—to learn new skills to be able to view and approach life differently. While the pandemic lay heavily on some for varied reasons, there were some who took this opportunity to focus on self-growth and build on their previous experiences; some even went ahead and tried working on an entirely different approach to reinvent themselves. The same can be seen in the game of Panch Kone. While some get frustrated and walk away, some try to fine-tune their previous approach or find an entirely new one.

I am reminded of the story of a feisty 89-year-old man, who had been running a vibrant and successful book club for a couple of years before the pandemic hit. To some, it may have seemed trivial, but to him it was an important aspect of his life—it defined him in many ways and he took pride in how effectively, efficiently and creatively he ran the club. He approached each meeting with new ideas to keep the members engaged and enthused. Once the pandemic hit, they could not meet anymore. But he refused to be fazed by this. He decided to have an online meet. To many of us, it might seem an obvious solution, but to an 89-year-old who had spent his childhood in an era when electricity was a luxury, learning to use online applications effectively so the meeting could go on smoothly required a lot of effort and time. But he persevered and conducted numerous mock meetings with friends and family before announcing his online book club meeting. His thorough preparation and understanding not only led to a perfectly curated meeting but he was actually able to guide numerous members who, though many years his junior, were not as tech-savvy as him.

Not every success story makes headlines and not every failure breaks the bank. It is our approach towards continuous improvement or reinvention of the self in the smallest of ways that makes us who we are.

In 1990, a small company in the city of Chennai decided to foray into the field of information technology. It was a time when computers were just making their way into the Indian market. This company had been running for almost 20 years in a completely different field, which was not proving to be too lucrative. The management decided that this new venture might be profitable. Two gleaming new computers were purchased and placed lovingly in an air-conditioned room. And soon came the time to train the employees. The reactions of five employees in particular are of interest as they mirror in many ways people's approach to the game of Panch Kone and life itself.

The first employee took one look at the computers, decided that the effort was too daunting and resigned from the company. This was similar to an incident I remember: a young man stopped at an event to ask about the game of Panch Kone, and when I gave him the details of the rules and the guidelines, he backed away shaking his head, without trying a single move. He was convinced he would fail and the lack of faith he had in himself led him to give up without even trying.

The second employee cautiously approached the management. He understood their direction and was interested, but really did not want to venture into learning as he was content with the knowledge he possessed and the role he had. The management cautioned him—he would lose seniority and his salary may not increase by much. But he was comfortable with that. And so, he continued in the company for 30 years till retirement, working on the fringes, but happy and content to be a spectator. This was akin to the people who come by to watch the game of Panch Kone at every event, sit for hours watching others play, learning just a little bit from other players, content in just being a spectator. Life is flowing past them, but they lack the courage to take the chance, to try something new. However, they are there to encourage and support all those who do.

The third employee took the plunge and decided to learn the skills needed to grow. And grow he did for many years. But about a decade or so down the road, his organization decided to reinvent itself again. At that point, he threw up his hands and could not find the effort needed to learn and grow again. He stagnated in his role, but nonetheless completed his career at the organization, eventually retiring at the age of 60. He reminds me of the player who is able to solve one version after several attempts, but gives up when confronted with another version, stepping aside for the next player.

The fourth employee was neither enamoured by the idea of learning how to use the computer, nor was he prepared to step aside. He kept growing frustrated with each passing day. His frustration turned toxic for the company, at which point he was let go. Many players exhibit the same trait. They do not play, but try to advise those who do. If someone succeeds, they do not celebrate the success, and instead attribute it to luck or a single input from themselves. Perhaps of all the examples, he is the one who has failed the most as he neither recognizes his limitations, nor is he willing to celebrate the success of another. His frustration became detrimental to his growth and infected the very environment till he was let go.

The fifth employee chose to learn and grow. He chose to reinvent himself again and again, and when the time came to retire, the organization urged him to stay on, and so he did as the chief financial officer. He reminds me of this senior management professional, greying at the temples, who came by and studied the game at an event. With a courteous 'May I?' he took the board and game pieces, and retreated to a corner, playing the game repeatedly, unbothered by the chaos around him till he finally cracked the code in the stars and played a perfect game.

The Symbolism of Panch Kone

Every game of Panch Kone is symbolic of the Hindu cycle of birth, death and rebirth. You try again and again until you achieve the goal of the game or moksha. And much like the cycle of birth and rebirth, you have to do it alone. This cycle is a solitary one, it is a journey you make on your own, again echoing the very ethos of the single-player game.

In Hindu philosophy, time has no beginning or end. It is a cycle repeating itself. In every beginning, there is an end, and in every end, there is a beginning. This philosophy expresses itself in the game in numerous ways. Firstly, the star itself. The ability to draw the star in a single unbroken line without breaks and pauses in many ways echoes this very concept of time. There is no beginning in the drawing of the star, there is no end, but only a single unbroken line. You can trace the star again and again without stopping or lifting your finger from the pattern.

Every game is like a lifetime in a microcosm, and each effort to improve and perfect the strategy in the game is equivalent to our journey towards moksha.

Interestingly, the clue to cracking the second version of the game lies in these very words—in every beginning, there is an end, and in every end, there is a beginning. To reveal the actual process will defeat the fun and purpose of this game.

H.G. Wells, the acclaimed English writer of novels and short stories, echoed this very concept when he said, 'Until a man has found God, he begins at no beginning and works to no end.' Whether we choose to define that ultimate achievement as finding God, moksha or perfection, the constant effort behind challenging oneself again and again in a cycle of continuous improvement is ingrained in our philosophy and in the very essence of the game of Panch Kone.

Section 2

....

STRATEGY

'You may never know what results will come from your action, but if you do nothing, there will be no results.'

—Mahatma Gandhi, Indian freedom fighter and lawyer

❖

Every aspect of our life requires thinking and strategic planning. Be it in our personal or professional life, this kind of planned approach is critical for success. Learning to think, make decisions, adapt, use and identify your resources, and take the initiative, be quick on your feet to respond are the traits of a strategic thinker.

Whether at home or in workplace, time and again, we find ourselves in a situation that requires us to strategize, plan and take action. The games in this section mimic many such life situations, which make you think strategically and plan your next move in a dynamic environment. It could be the wrong move, but you will never know until you try. And with every mistake, you learn to think better.

2

ASHTAA CHEMMAA[5]: WHEN CONCRETE ACTION LEADS TO ADVANCEMENT

The game of Ashtaa Chemmaa
Photo credit: Kreeda

---

[5]Also known as Eight and Four, *Kattam Kali, Chauka Baara, Changapoo, Ettu Veedu, Kattam Kazhi, Aada Sada*, etc.

Ashtaa Chemmaa is one of the numerous dice games popular across India. According to H.J.R. Murray, a British educationalist, inspector of schools and acclaimed chess historian, games like Ashtaa Chemmaa are considered cross and circle games, a subcategory of race games. In his book, *A History of Board-Games Other Than Chess* published in 1952, Murray, who is considered an authority on board games across the world, came up with a classification that we use even today.

Race games are those in which the object of the game is to reach the end before anyone else. While dice are used in most race games to define the movement of the game pieces, not all games that use dice are race games. Take for instance the game of Monopoly, which uses dice, but has no actual finish line. A win is not defined by speed, but the assets collected by the players. Thus, the games where the win is defined by the first person to reach the end are classified as race games.

Cross and circle games refer to a specific set of race games where there is an almost circular movement of game pieces on the boards as against, for example, the game of Parama Padam Sopanam or Snakes and Ladders. Hence, the game of Ashtaa Chemmaa is a cross and circle game played not with traditional dice, but with cowrie shells as throw pieces.

Understanding Dice

Firstly, let us understand dice. Dice are small throwable objects having multiple resting positions, which generate random numbers.

Gambling with dice finds mention even in the Vedas. When we say the word 'dice', we normally conjure up images of square dice with its faces marked from 1 to 6, or in some cases, the long dice that are popular in India. While these are the most common of all, there are several other related objects, shapes and devices that can be used for generating random numbers.

The most common objects used as dice are two-sided flat sticks, bamboo sticks cut in two, tamarind seeds cut in two and cowrie shells. Technically, any two-faced object, like an ordinary coin, can be referred to as a dice. The two-faced object can be tossed or thrown to randomly generate one of the two possible results.

Bamboo sticks cut in half to be used as throw pieces
Photo credit: Author

Cowrie shells
Photo credit: Kreeda

Animal bones, especially knuckle bones, were commonly used as dice in many ancient cultures, including those of the Egyptians, Romans and Greeks. Another common method of generating random results is to use a spinning wheel. This is notably found in casinos.

The 'Gambler's Lament' refers to the akṣa (gambling dice) made from nuts of *bibhitaki* (*terminalia bellirica*) with four scoring sides—kṛta (four), tretā (trey), dvāpar (deuce) and kali (ace). This hymn is presented as a monologue by a repentant gambler who laments the ruin brought on him because of his addiction to gambling: 'When the brown dice, thrown on the board, have rattled, like a fond girl I seek the place of meeting...' [6]

While many believe that the square dice is a modern concept or even a western import, that is, in fact, not true. Square terracotta dice have been found in the excavations of the Indus Valley. Some of the dice have 1 opposite 6, 2 opposite 5 and 3 opposite 4, so they add up to 7—much like the modern-day square dice. However, dice have also been found with other styles of numbering. Even as recently as 2021, archaeologists at the excavations in Keezhadi in Tamil Nadu have found square dice marked from 1 to 6. Experts date the excavated remains between fifth century BCE and third century CE.[7]

Long dice are yet another type of dice that are very popular in India. Oblong in shape, with markings on four faces, these dice are designed to land on any of the marked faces. In India, long dice may be marked with the values 1-3-4-6 or 1-2-5-6 or 1-2-3-4. In South India, the dice are marked 0-1-2-3 where 0 means 0 in combination with another number, but two 0s are taken as 12.

---

[6]Pillai, Madhavankutty, 'Why Do We Gamble?' *Open*, 29 October 2021, https://bit.ly/3pgN1we. Accessed on 25 February 2022.

[7]Express News Service, 'Ancient secrets: Terracotta die unearthed in Keezhadi', *The New Indian Express*, 18 April 2021, https://bit.ly/3LtvvxM. Accessed on 29 March 2022.

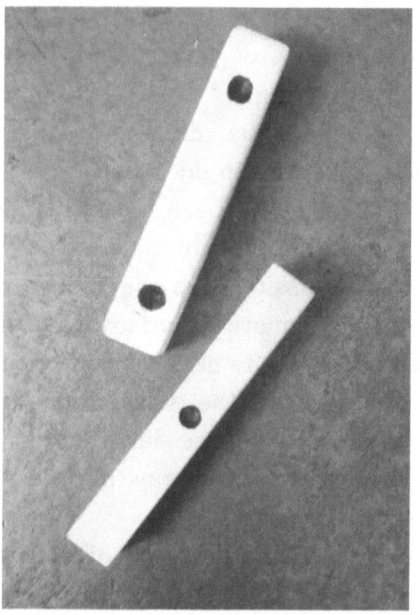

Long dice
Photo credit: Kreeda

It is incredible how much history we take for granted as far as these small pieces of wood and terracotta are concerned. It would be interesting to close our eyes hold a pair of dice in our hand and remember that at some point, thousands of years ago, someone just like us held similar dice in their hands and played a game.

The cowrie shells used as throw pieces in Ashtaa Chemmaa tell an interesting tale. Cowrie is the common name for sea snails and molluscs belonging to the Cypraeidae family. These shells have been used as currency, as well as in the making of jewellery and for other decorative purposes because of their porcelain-like appearance, which makes them look attractive. Interestingly, the Italian name for cowrie is porcellana, which is actually the root of the word 'porcelain'!

Ashtaa Chemmaa is played with four cowries. When one shell falls open-faced, it is counted as 1, when two shells fall open faced, it is counted as 2, when three shells fall open-faced, it is counted as 3 and four open-faced shells are counted as 4 or *chemmaa* in Telugu. When all shells fall closed, it is counted as 8 or *ashtaa*. Thus, the game pieces can be moved by throwing 1-2-3-4-8.

A few years ago, I received a mail from a concerned environmentalist. 'Cowries are actually animals (living molluscs) that are harvested, killed and then sold for their shell value. Their population numbers are dropping steadily. They are a vital part of the coral reef ecosystems of the world. In our work in the Andaman and Nicobar Islands and Lakshadweep, we have actively sought to ban cowrie collection and use. I am sure you will agree that it is a wise thing to replace them with other sustainable products...'

As concerned citizens, I believe that while it is important to preserve our games, it is equally important for us to take efforts to find sustainable alternatives to preserve our biodiversity as well.

While Ashtaa Chemmaa is native to the Telugu heartland, the game is played across the country in almost the same way. The difference is usually in the number of cowries and the kind of dice used. The board of Ashtaa Chemmaa is usually a 5x5 square board, though large boards with more rows of squares can also be found.

How Do You Play?

Each player has four game pieces and starts on a different side of the board at the square marked with an X. With the throw of the cowries, the players move each of their game pieces all the way around the board in a clockwise direction. When they return to the home square, they graduate to the inner band, where they move around in an anticlockwise direction. Once they have completed a circuit of the inner band, they can enter the centre square, which is the final destination. The challenge is for each game piece to reach the final destination without being killed. An opponent can kill a game piece by simply landing on it. Squares marked with an X are safe spaces where you cannot be killed. The inner band has no safe spaces. The first player to guide all of his four game pieces safely to the final destination or innermost square becomes the winner.

And here comes the twist in the game—before entering the inner band, a player must kill at least one game piece of the opponent. If not, he has to circle again and again till he kills one.

After the player completes the necessary task of killing a game piece of an opponent and moving to the inner band, he is faced with another twist in the game. While movement on the outside band was in the clockwise direction, movement in the inner one has to be in the anti-clockwise direction. This complete change of direction, though simple in a game, can be unnerving if it were a real-life scenario.

This game of Ashtaa Chemmaa was found inscribed on the floor of the Kapaleeswarar Temple in Mylapore, Chennai in 2009. Sadly during renovations, the board seems to have disappeared.
Photo credit: Kreeda

While at one level, the game is a wonderful way to pass time, losing ourselves in fun and laughter, there are fascinating lessons within its rules that can well impact the way we view our life.

Decisive Actions

Perhaps the first and most critical lesson we learn is the need to take a decisive action. The player has to kill one game piece of the opponent in order to advance to the inner band. There are some who frown upon this requirement. However, one cannot and should not consider this a celebration of violence. Instead, the act of killing or cutting symbolizes a decisive action necessary to take the player to the next level.

In life, there is a need to overcome or defeat the opposition as a stepping stone to success. Success and failure are two sides of the same coin. Without failure, the concept of success cannot exist. Human beings across the world want to be happy and succeed. These are the dreams, hopes and aspirations that all of us harbour throughout our lives. The only thing that differs is our definition of success. Success for one may be creating a beautiful piece of art, for another it could be coping with the challenges of a family and for someone else, it could be the desire to build a reputed organization.

All of these, nonetheless, require a certain amount of effort. And this effort comes with the need for a decision that enables better performance, progress and the ability to prevail. A college student may need to be decisive in his choice of subject or selection of college, a young woman may need to take decisions on balancing her responsibilities in office and at home, an executive may need to prioritize among the various issues he is confronted with on the job front. They all require a decisive action.

A friend of mine, who was a senior executive in a large company, was excellent at his work and was given the opportunity to move to the head office in a different city. He felt honoured and knew that he would now be on the fast track for getting more senior positions. However, he had a family—his children were well-settled in school and his wife ran a successful business. He chose to let go of the promotion. Although difficult, it was a decisive move. The consequences were his to accept. And while this decisiveness may or may not have helped his career, it kept the family together. Thus, every decisive action takes us to the next step, but only time can tell what the next step will bring. It is often not the decision that matters but the need to be decisive, for without that, we would circle endlessly like the player, who goes round and round without entering the inner band.

What is Decisiveness?

Decisiveness is the ability to make decisions or take action without losing time. On finding an ambiguous test result of a patient, a doctor often has to take a quick and difficult decision, which will further define the course of treatment given to the patient, whose life might depend on it. The captain of a cricket team has to be decisive in his approach, when it comes to the choice of bowler, field positioning and almost every aspect of the game.

Making decisions is a part of life. These could be trivial or critical, could lead to success or failure, or merely define the next step, but each one of them counts as a decision. The clothes we choose to wear, the food we choose to eat, the job we choose to take up and the things we choose to not do are all part of an elaborate decision-making process.

Change Is the Only Constant

In the harum-scarum world of the twenty-first century, change seems to be the one constant in life. As we explore new ideas, new dreams or new countries, there are certain situations we cannot control, and that in turn force us to change.

With global markets opening up, organizations are now competing with the best the world has to offer. The need to constantly update oneself, to reinvent oneself by learning new ideas, to learn to face new competition and adapt to change in the environment is the need of the hour. Organizations or individuals who do not change and adapt are left behind.

A long-term employee of an organization was greatly responsible for its growth from a tiny five-man team to almost 100 employees. A natural salesman, he was good at his job. But as the organization grew, it became necessary to set up systems to cope with the growth, to track performance and ensure a cohesive functioning of the company. Unfortunately, he could not accept these changes. He fought them, refused to accept them and over a period of time, he was left behind, unhappy and disgruntled. He ultimately chose to leave the organization.

A project was conceived under the umbrella of a large well-funded NGO to monitor and counsel vulnerable children living in far-flung villages across a state. After a successful run for two years, the NGO chose to withdraw operations from the state. The management of the project had a problem on their hands now. If they chose to continue with the project, where would the funds come from? And most important of all, would the funds be sufficient to cover the cost of counsellor visits to the children scattered across the state?

Faced with this sudden change, the management was compelled to make numerous decisions. It required a change in thinking and devising innovative solutions if the project was to survive. An interesting idea that came up in discussion seemed to hold the answers. It was the height of the telecom boom and everyone had a phone. It was proposed that telephone counselling could perhaps hold the answer to the questions. It was not without its drawbacks and risks. The personal touch would be missing. Phone numbers changed constantly as people sought cheaper and better plans. Connectivity became a challenge.

However, as this was the only option that held some answers, the management decided to embrace the change, for which new plans were framed.

A decade later, the management could look back and call the effort an outstanding success. What started as a change became the perfect formula for functioning. Phone counselling was far less expensive and the frequency of contact mitigated the loss of the personal touch. The flexibility of access meant counsellors were available round the clock to deal with potential issues. And as the impact of the calls was realized, beneficiaries took it upon themselves to inform the team about the change in numbers. Over a period of time, children in far-flung villages, with counselling, learned to cope with their challenges and began to build successful lives of their own.

These examples show that change, which has always been a part of our lives, only goes on to increase with time, as we deal with new cultures, new people and new ideas.

Interestingly, in the inner band of Ashtaa Chemmaa,

not only do we change direction, we also find there are no safe spaces, thereby denoting a higher risk of being cut or killed by your opponent. Even in real life, change comes with risk. However, if we learn to cope, we can succeed and finally see a win.

Change is the only constant. We cannot define it or choose it. It is defined and chosen for us as is the board and the rules that govern it. What we can do is accept it, learn to cope with it and even embrace it as a way to grow as individuals and slowly make our way to the finishing point in the game.

3

SOLAH SEEDI:[8] STRATEGIC THINKING TO ACHIEVE YOUR GOAL

The game of Solah Seedi
Photo credit: Kreeda

At one level, the game of *Solah Seedi* is a simple one. There is a board, there are two players with an equal number of game pieces and the objective of each player is to occupy the territory of the opponent while defending his own. How

---

[8]Also known as *Vettai, Athara Seiya, Goti ka Khel*, etc.

this is achieved does not matter. It can be done either by killing all the pieces of the opponent or by outsmarting the opponent and slipping through the gaps. The choice is up to the player.

Although the game is called Solah Seedi or 16 pieces, there are many versions of the game, and the number of game pieces varies in each. The game is played on a square board with two triangular extensions. But there is no restraint to the creativity of the human mind. Game designers from ancient times have created numerous boards using variations of this design. Thus, you can find boards with four, eight or even more triangular extensions. There is one version that even does away with the square and has just two triangles facing each other. Each version builds on the complexities of the game, but for the purposes of this chapter, we will focus on the square board with two triangular extensions.

Game with four triangular extensions inscribed on the floor of Thiyagarajaswamy Temple at Thiruvottriyur, Chennai
Photo credit: Author

However, it is variations like these that make the study of traditional games a complex yet fascinating one. Every board has to be studied so as to understand if it is a variation of a game or an entirely different one. As if this complexity was not enough, games are known by different names in different parts of the country. This can be confusing because we could have just figured out the ins and outs of a game when someone comes up with a new name, which we would have never heard before. And then we are left scratching our heads, wondering if it is a new name for a game we have come to know or a completely new game.

Then there is yet another aspect that can confuse us. Traditionally, people were so creative that they played different games on the same board. So, we might be seeing the exact same board we know from a game, but then someone tells us about a completely different game that used to be played on it. We will never exactly know which game was actually played.

Discovering the rules of a game is yet another challenge. As most rules were never written down, discovering how to play traditional games requires a lot of effort. Digging through old books helps, of course, but most books merely mention names and don't detail the rules well enough for us to play. So we are often left with huge gaps or questions. We might try talking to people, particularly senior citizens who are storehouses of our country's culture, but sadly, many games are dying out from living memory.

I like to think of it as some kind of a quest. And just like the heroes of yore who went out to seek a treasure or a key to a puzzle, the discovery of traditional games is a treasure in itself too.

Discovering and putting together a traditional game is not any less challenging. The obstacles are numerous, the clues obscure, and it requires dedication and commitment to overcome all the obstacles and finally piece the rules of the game together. The journey is sometimes as interesting as the game itself. If we are lucky, we will find the right people to guide us, we will decipher the clues, and then like pieces of a jigsaw puzzle we can put it all together and test it.

As explained before, this game has two opponents, equal in strength, pitted against one another in an effort to conquer enemy territory. If we think of this game as life in miniature, occupying enemy territory is symbolic of the goal we wish to achieve; the rival, our opponent, is symbolic of the obstacles on the way to achieve it. So what matters is our strategy. Do we methodically kill our opponent's pieces? Do we wait for gaps to sneak in? Do we focus more on protecting or defending our own territory rather than attacking our opponent?

Strategy is a matter of approach. What works in one situation may not work in another. What works for one person may not work for another. Take the example of two young women who joined an organization as the next step in their career. They joined at about the same time and in the same team. The team lead was a rather difficult woman who had risen through the ranks and proved herself to be an invaluable asset to the company. She was demanding of the new recruits, unforgiving when they made mistakes and altogether a difficult boss.

The two young women approached the problem differently. The first woman decided to take the challenge head-on. She plunged right into work with grit and determination that often pitted her against her boss, but she accepted every challenge and outperformed many others, so she could rise through the ranks. The boss did not like her, but could not stop her, as her tactics were aggressive, yet effective.

The second young woman tried a different approach. She worked closely with her boss, shadowing her, learning from her and biding time till an opportunity presented itself. At the end of three years, both women were team leads, both had achieved their goals. The difference was in the strategy they adopted to get there.

So How Do You Play?

The game of Solah Seedi has 37 points on the board created by the intersection or meeting point of lines. Each player has 16 game pieces. Before the start of the game, they are placed on opposite ends of the board leaving the centre row of five points empty. The game pieces can then move along the lines either to the next empty space or by jumping over the opponent's piece to an empty space, thus killing that piece. The aim, as mentioned before, is to reach and occupy the far point on the triangle of the opponent, while defending our own.

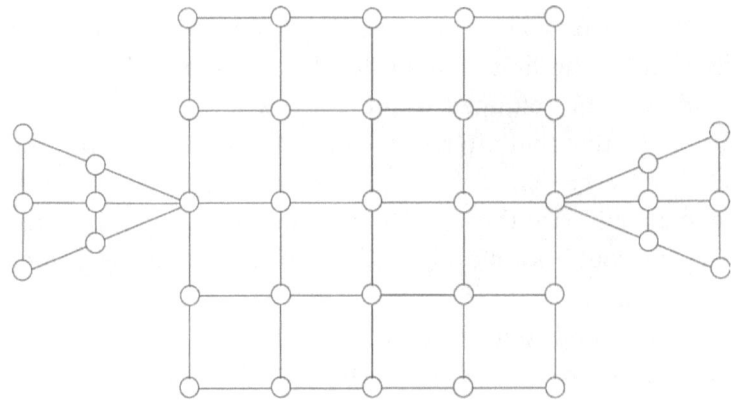

Illustration of the game of Solah Seedi
Illustration credit: Kreeda

While starting the game, the empty row in the centre gives some room to manoeuvre and attempt a few moves to hone our strategy against the opponent. It also gives us time to try and figure out the other person's strategy.

There is one version of the game, wherein each player has 18 pieces. When they are placed on the board before the game starts, only one point in the centre is left empty. This means the game is a battle from the word 'go', requiring players to be quick in their thinking to protect their territory. There is no time to understand the opponent, no time to hone strategy, no time at all, we just have to do it.

It is the strategic thinking that makes it an abstract strategy game. A strategy game is one in which the independent decision-making skill of the players has an extensive relationship with the outcome or the result of the game. In an abstract strategy game, the theme is not relevant to the experience of the game.

J. Mark Thompson in his article, 'Defining the Abstract', wrote: 'There is an intimate relationship between such games and puzzles: every board position presents the player with the puzzle. What is the best move, which in theory could be solved by logic alone? A good abstract game can therefore be thought of as a "family" of potentially interesting logic puzzles, and the play consists of each player posing such a puzzle to the other. Good players are the ones who find the most difficult puzzles to present to their opponents.'[9]

In the business scenario, the best-known clash of this kind is the Cola Wars.[10] This refers to the long-time rivalry between soft drink producers—The Coca-Cola Company and PepsiCo. Their mutually targeted marketing efforts and innovative advertising techniques to corner the market share was much like a strategy game of Solah Seedi: each opponent throwing a new twist or approach into the game forces the other to innovate, respond and counteract in order to defeat the opponent.

Interestingly, a series of puzzles is often the framework for a quest. The ones who can solve the puzzles or overcome the obstacles get through the quest.

In the Hindu epic, Ramayana, when Hanuman offered to leap across the ocean and search for Sita in Lanka, he was confronted by numerous obstacles and challenges. But his determination, courage, wit and wisdom enabled him to

---

[9]Mark Thompson, J., 'Defining the Abstract', *The Games Journal*, July 2000, https://bit.ly/3pqmuwD. Accessed on 28 February 2022.

[10]Domanska, Anna, 'The Cola Wars Timeline: What Went Down', *Industry Leaders*, https://bit.ly/3pmXNBr. Accessed on 28 February 2022.

overcome them all. Whether it was the mighty mountain Mynaaka, who offered him a place to rest, or Surasa, the demon who insisted he enter her mouth, or Simhika, who tried to hold him back—nothing stopped him from his goal. What is interesting to note is that not all obstacles were evil or destructive. Mynaaka, for example, merely offered Hanuman a place to rest. Understanding that obstacles can come in numerous forms, the latter was not deterred from his goal. So, often in life when we are set on a goal, we understand the obstacles and challenges, but we succumb to the gentle distractions and the compulsions to take it easy or give up when the road ahead seems challenging.

Perfect Information

There is another aspect of the game that should be understood. In game theory, it is referred to as a game with perfect information. This phrase has its origins in economics where 'perfect information' refers to a market where all consumers and producers have perfect and instantaneous knowledge of all market prices, their own utility, own cost functions—in other words all information is out in the open.

In a game, each player, when making any decision, is perfectly informed of all the events that have previously occurred, including the 'initialization event' of the game, or the starting point of the game. Another example of a game with perfect information is chess as each player can see all the pieces on the board at all times. In many ways, this is an ideal situation. Although there is an opponent blocking our way, we are evenly matched, our goals mirror his, our game pieces mirror his and the board is an open book. There is no hidden information. The tools are the same, the goals are the same—it is one mind pitted against another. Thus, the need of the hour is to ensure that our mental skills, our ability to think strategically, our ability to analyse every move is better than the opponent's. If we lose, it is not luck, it is not situations beyond our control, it is not the unknown that is responsible, but our own inability to outsmart the opponent. What is more, we need to clearly understand the information before us. If we misread it, if we choose to ignore information, or if we do not understand it completely, our moves too will be wrong. Understanding and using the knowledge we have is critical.

Knowledge Management

Knowledge management is the process of creating, sharing, using and managing knowledge and information, and the steps taken to achieve objectives by making the best use of available knowledge. When we take a knowledge-based decision, we are better equipped to take responsibility for it.

A boy, being supported by an NGO, had long dreamt of becoming a doctor. He came from a small village, and saw the role of doctor as glamorous and heroic. When it came to his final year of school and his applications, he was determined to apply for medicine and nothing else. Unfortunately, despite all his interest and passion, he did not have the requisite marks. Over the years, he had been an average student who was unable to put in the necessary hard work and pick up his grades. However, he was blinded by his dreams and was not willing to see the writing on the wall. The NGO was loath to destroy his dreams, but knew that he would not qualify for the admission. They were worried about how he would react on learning he had failed in his efforts.

One person, though, had the bright idea of taking him to a large hospital and encouraging him to interact with the staff. As he came to know that a hospital had numerous people working in it, with each one playing a different role as important as the doctors, he became more amenable to reason. He applied for a course to train as a physician's assistant. Today, he is employed in a large hospital, draws a good salary and is able to support his family. Once he had a clear understanding of the options before him, once he saw things as they were, he was able to take a decision that would suit him best. The decision was his to take.

However, there are numerous times in life when we know the facts before us, but take wrong decisions, and later blame the consequences on fate and luck. True, there are situations beyond our control, but in many of them, like the game of Solah Seedi, it is a situation of perfect information. Everything is laid out before us. All we must do is see it, understand it and then make a move. Sometimes we don't see it, just like the young boy in the story who did not see his limitations.

Life is like that. There are situations that are clear to us. It is how we handle them that matters. The game gives us a chance to practise that methodical strategic approach again and again without fearing lasting consequences, for when it comes to life there are rarely second chances. Every scenario in life is fraught with obstacles—small, big and complex ones. A planned and well-thought-out approach, with every possible effort in strategic planning, anticipation, mental agility and resourcefulness makes achieving the goals easier.

Utilizing Resources Effectively

In some ways, Solah Seedhi is reminiscent of war games. Think about it. A player has to occupy enemy territory and needs the strategy to back up his efforts. Another fascinating aspect of the game is that a player can win with just one game piece occupying enemy territory and yet has 16 pieces to help him achieve this. The effective player uses his resources wisely, directing the move of every piece, so that one game piece finally reaches the end point in the opponent's side of the board. This again is reminiscent of a general using his resources wisely in war, for unused or poorly used resources only weaken the position. But while the theme is dominant, that is not the whole story. There is more to this game than just war and in it we find situations that mirror our life situations that teach us how to act, react and achieve our goals.

A young mother was trying to maintain a balance between her home and career. It was a challenge. The children needed time, her parents and in-laws needed time and she needed time to deliver her professional commitments. As time went by and she tried doing everything herself, the situation became more and more impossible. Frustration set in and she found that she was never happy. When she worked, she felt she was neglecting the family and vice versa.

This dilemma, as a result of a never-ending balancing act, is faced by many women. Those who have overcome this successfully are the ones who have realized that the goals may be theirs alone, but the resources to achieve the same can be numerous.

This young mother sat down and took stock of her life. What could she change? She could seek help—from her family to help with the children, from the grandparents to spend time with them, read to them and play with them. She could seek her husband's help and give him greater responsibility. She could seek the help of friends. She could also relook at her life and change the way she did things. She could compromise on things that did not matter and let go of those that were less important. She could make use of her time while the children were busy playing or when they were asleep. She could use technology to monitor things and simplify her life. She could hire help.

Despite the changes she made, life remained a balancing act and there were still times when she felt guilty. But she no longer felt alone. She still had her goals, but now she knew that she was making the best use of her resources to reach the goals. The resources we have are ours to use—the support of family, the help of friends, even our own ability to think and do things differently, to adapt and to change our behaviour. These are the resources we have and if we deploy them properly and use them wisely, overcoming obstacles can become a tad easier with the goal becoming more reachable.

Every game is a microcosm of life. In every move, there is a lesson for us. If there were no obstacles, the very charm of the game would be lost. We see that clearly. Without the opponent, without the challenges, without the obstacles, there is no game. Yet, we expect life to flow without opposition, without challenges and obstacles. That is an unreal expectation. What we need is not a life without challenges but one where we develop the strength and tools to cope, to overcome and succeed.

4

KATTAM VILAYATTU:[11] STRATEGIES IN BEING PROACTIVE AND REACTIVE

Close your eyes and go back in time—school, ragged notebooks, all the wonderful games you played with friends, a teacher standing near a chalkboard teaching math, or maybe history, students bent over their books taking notes, and somewhere two seemingly serious students with inky hands and dirty faces bent over a book in concentration, playing a game. Remember the game of Noughts and Crosses with X and O marked alternately on a grid to get three in a row?

It would be interesting to study how many games of Noughts and Crosses have been played on the back pages of schoolbooks. There would be that one friend who would win all the time, or another friend with whom we were equally matched and every game would end in a draw. It was definitely more interesting than the lesson being taught in the classroom!

---

[11]Also known as Tic Tac Toe, Noughts and Crosses, *Teen Goti/Char Goti*, etc.

It is perhaps the most simplistic of three-in-a-row games—a game played mostly by young children—and often leads to a draw when both players put their best foot forward.

It seems rather simple and yet it was the subject of study by John Forbes Nash Jr, an American mathematician whose significant contributions to game theory, differential geometry and the study of partial differential equations is well known throughout the world. Nash's work gives us some insight into the various factors that govern chance and decision-making.

In a two-player game, if each player has chosen the best strategy based on what has happened so far in the game and cannot improve their chances of winning, by changing their strategy, as long as the strategy of the other player is unchanged, then the current set of strategic choices is called a Nash equilibrium.

Let us try to simplify this. Let us assume you sit down with a childhood friend and decide to play Noughts and Crosses. You choose strategy A and your friend chooses strategy B. If A is the best strategy for you against your friend's strategy B, and B is the best strategy for him against your strategy A, then (A, B) is the Nash equilibrium!

Three-in-a-row games or games of alignment like Noughts and Crosses are popular all over the world and they have been around long enough to leave their impact on thinkers of the calibre of John Nash. It also means that simple childhood games are rooted in science and strategic concepts that could well influence our thinking in real life.

The Fascination with Three-in-a-row

While Noughts and Crosses usually ends in a draw when both players are evenly matched, India has a whole range of traditional three-in-a-row games that require you to play to a conclusion. But before we go on to understand these games, or how they are played, perhaps it would be interesting to understand why there are so many three-in-a-row games around the world. Picaria, Three Men's Morris, Achi, Nine Holes, Shisima, Tapatan, the list goes on and on. So, what is the fascination with three-in-a-row?

The number 3 has a long history of mythical associations. The triple deity is commonly known in the world of mythology. From Zeus (Greek king of the gods), Athena (Greek goddess of war and intellect) and Apollo (Greek god of the sun, culture and music) to Osiris (Egyptian god of the underworld), Isis (his wife) and Horus (son), the concept of a triad in mythologies across the world is well-known. Even the reference to the Father, Son and the Holy Ghost encapsulates the number 3. Closer to home, it is echoed in the Hindu trinity of Brahma, Vishnu and Shiva.

From a mathematical perspective, three is an interesting number. It is the smallest odd prime number and the only prime preceding a square number, 4. The number 2 is the only even prime number and there are only two consecutive natural numbers which are prime—2 and 3. Just to continue with the flashback of school, in case you were not paying attention during classes, a prime number is a whole number greater than 1 that cannot be exactly divided by any whole number other than itself.

When we look at it from the point of view of alignment, a penny drops. Two game pieces placed on a board are naturally aligned. When we introduce a third, the alignment is destroyed. Bringing three game pieces into a straight line balances that alignment. This is interestingly reflected in the concept of the three gunas—*sattva*, *rajas* and *tamas* (harmony, energy and inertia). According to an ancient belief, the three gunas are three modes of existence, or the three aspects of nature, and are present in all things in the universe.

In order for humans to live a meaningful life, all three gunas are needed. Sattva is required to attain knowledge, happiness and peace of mind. Rajas is required to maintain the body and keep the mind alert. Tamas is needed to rest the body and mind. These three gunas should be in proper proportions, or in other words, perfectly aligned for a balanced life.

While the games of alignment may not be based on the concepts of the three gunas, it is fascinating to note the mystical properties of the number 3 and how it has penetrated the most simplistic of our childhood games.

I have always believed, and the more I read, the more convinced I am that even the simplest of games draw inspiration from our environment, culture, thinking and mythology.

While three-in-a-row games are perhaps the most popular of the games of alignment, there are numerous games that require four-in-a-row or even five-in-a-row.

Similarity Across the World

This similarity of games across the world in seemingly unconnected places is fascinating. Many of the games we believe are traditional or unique to India often have parallels or similarities with games played elsewhere. Did they develop simultaneously in different parts of the world? If games are a response to human thought, philosophy and the environment, it is likely that this creative response could be similar in different places.

Did the games get exchanged along trade routes? Travel in traditional times was not the one-day affair it is today. It took months, even years to travel across countries. Families went along and interacted with the locals, probably passing the time by playing together. We could well imagine a caravan stopping on a lonely outpost in the night, oil lamps flickering in the breeze, the visitors and locals trying hard to communicate through signs, with the language perhaps being unknown. And then after a meal, they settle down to play a game, for most of these games need no language— they are basic and intrinsic. Or perhaps a group of ragged children meet with the visitors and bond like children always do over fun, laughter, mischief and a game. The visitors might move on some days later, but they carry with them the memory of the game. They might add their own rules, teach their own people and over time, it may get entrenched in their culture. We will never know for sure, but the fact remains that similar games are found across the world.

Why Alignment?

Race games, hunt games and battlefield games reflect the human impulse, actions and physical behaviour. But why alignment? What does it reflect?

Sociologist Erving Goffman says, 'Aligning action in any behaviour indicates to others the acceptance of a particular definition of the situation, while a realigning action is an attempt to change the definition of the situation.'[12] Sociologists recognize that people do a lot of unseen work in their interactions with others. Much of that work is about agreeing to or challenging what sociologists call 'the definition of the situation'.

The 'definition of the situation' is based on social norms and must be understood by all for smooth social interaction. As per Goffman, an aligning action is something a person does to indicate that they agree with the existing definition of the situation, while a realigning action challenges or tries to change the social norms.[13]

Some of these can be very commonplace, such as standing in a queue or talking softly in a place of worship. In the multicultural world we live in, the response to social norms that differ from place to place often creates friction. For example, many homes in India expect you to remove your shoes on entering. However, people raised in a different culture may fail to do so, leading to feelings of discomfort.

---

[12]Crossman, Ashley, 'How Our Aligning Behavior Shapes Everyday Life', *ThoughtCo*, 6 November 2020, https://bit.ly/3MfemZB. Accessed on 1 March 2022.
[13]Ibid.

As the world grows smaller and intercultural interactions increase, the need to understand cultures and avoid unplanned realigning actions becomes more and more crucial for social peace. Planned realigning actions tell those around us that we are breaking from norms because we believe that the norms that define a situation are wrong, unjust, immoral or just plain unnecessary. This could range from the simplest of actions, such as a teenager who chooses to sport a tattoo or a mohawk, to the civil disobedience movement during the freedom struggle of India.

As human interaction is as old as life itself, the importance given to alignment could well be rooted in the human desire for peace and balance.

Teen Goti or Kattam Vilayattu

This game of alignment has a simple beginning. What makes it different from Noughts and Crosses is that after the placement of three pieces on the board by each player, the pieces can be moved around. The game continues until there is a result. While one version of the game allows you to move along the diagonals, the other does not. The game is meant to be fast-paced, forcing players to think quickly and avoid error under pressure.

Three-in-a-row game that allows you to move along the diagonals
Photo credit: Kreeda

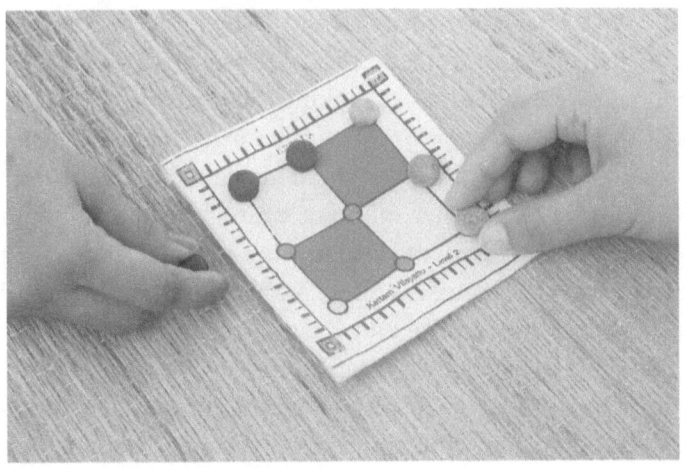

Three-in-a-row game that does not allow you
to move along the diagonals
Photo credit: Kreeda

When we drive a car in traffic, we take a number of decisions quickly. With cars, trucks, cycles, motorbikes, pedestrians and even cows on the road, these decisions are often fraught with tension, but with years of practice, we have trained ourselves to react almost subconsciously to these situations.

Many years ago, there was a young schoolboy who was prone to injury. He was active and adventurous, which led him to suffer scrapes, bruises, fractures and sprains. After a particularly boisterous game of football, he complained of pain in his neck. Most people took it lightly and told him to rub a balm and move on. After all, here was a boy who always injured himself and there really did not seem anything much wrong with him. However, a doctor on call made a quick decision to immobilize the neck. When questioned later, she was unsure why she took that decision, after all his description of the pain was like every other injury. However, her quick thinking saved the day. A hairline fracture in the neck was prevented from getting worse before it could widen and cause permanent damage. In this case, the doctor relied on her inherent training in medicine, but there are times when the situation is unusual and fraught with unexpected consequences. We are not prepared, we do not have the knowledge, and yet a decision must be taken.

A short while ago, I met someone who said he was witness to a terrorist attack. After spending hours hiding, he decided to slip out and try to escape. There seemed to be a small window of opportunity. He chose to go left instead of right and after wandering a bit reached a small exit from where he could escape. It was a quick decision and for years later, he wondered what would have happened had he gone right instead of left.

In life, there are times when we need the ability to analyse a situation at a glance, think quickly and react effectively. Life decisions could have far-reaching consequences and the ability to make a quick decision is an important component of any strategy.

Chaar Goti

An interesting and unusual version is this game that requires the player to get four (chaar) game pieces in a row. This makes for an exciting and nail-biting game of strategy where each player tries to outwit the other.

A four-in-a-row game
Photo credit: Kreeda

The strategy for this game is critical because there are two distinct stages—a proactive stage and a reactive stage. First comes the proactive stage, where the player initially positions each game piece on the basis of a plan. This envisages not only what he will do but also how he has planned to counter what the opponent is likely to do. The second level of strategy comes into play when all the pieces are on the board. At that stage, the players try to outwit each other to reach the objective. The first-stage moves take place under unknown conditions and are open-ended as the player has the freedom to place the game piece anywhere. This stage could quite often determine the chances of success and calls for imagination and anticipation. The way the game pieces are placed in the first stage could confer positional advantages or act as constraints. The second stage is under known conditions, but the moves are constrained by the opponent's positioning. Thus, we are taught to think under two different sets of conditions as it happens often in life.

While the game pieces are being laid out, each player places them based on his own inner thinking and strategy. But once the players start moving pieces, the thinking must change. The moves of the players are thus influenced by the moves of the opponent.

There are no dice in this game and as such there is no element of chance. The determinants of success are sound tactical plans, anticipation and the ability to make swift changes to the tactical plan in order to cope with the constraints in the environment and the opposing player's counter moves.

*The game of Char Goti inscribed on the floor of Kapaleeswarar Temple
in Mylapore, Chennai. This was documented in 2009,
but due to subsequent renovations,
this board can no longer be found at the temple.
Photo credit: Kreeda*

Many of our decisions and efforts are taken based on
our approach and thinking towards a situation. However,
when the situation changes, the decisions and actions of

other people force us to rethink our strategy and adapt in real time.

An extremely creative young woman established a small business of making exquisitely designed boxes out of paper and cardboard. Over the years, her business attracted numerous customers looking for creative packaging solutions for gifts exchanged in weddings, festivals and functions. She employed six women to help her with the business and trained them in their craft. Things were going well till 2020. Then the pandemic changed the world as we knew it. Large weddings and functions became a thing of the past and with sales dropping, this young woman was left struggling to pay the bills.

She could perhaps have shut down the business since she did not depend on it for her bread and butter, but it was her baby and she had nurtured it over the years. She was sure it was a matter of time before life slowly drifted back to normal, but how could she sustain it in the interim? She also had six employees, who had no other source of income, and depended on her; she could not bear the thought of letting them go.

She looked around and realized that with the lockdown restrictions in place, there was a greater demand for delivery services. Many home bakers and restaurants needed paper bags to have food delivered. Since she worked with paper, she diversified into making bags. It did not give her the creative outlet that making gift boxes offered, but it paid the bills and kept her afloat to tide over the tough times, while ensuring that the women who worked for her also had money to make ends meet.

This ability to react to the environment, to modify our plans and our approach in the face of changes in the environment or the actions of others, becomes critical to our everyday lives. These elements are well illustrated by this game. Alignment of pieces is equivalent to the prerequisite of synchronizing our resources and tactical moves before tackling a situation. This is a game of anticipation. In life, there is continuous interface with the environment and other people. Their responses are outside our control but can be predicted with insight. Dealing with another person's reactions and the environment are the key to success and good strategic planning.

Section 3

··

SYNERGY

'Alone we can do so little; together we can do so much.'

—Helen Keller, American author and
disability rights activist

❖

Synergy is critical to success. Synergy is not merely teamwork, but the coming together of people, resources and ideas. It is a community where each one looks out for and supports the other. It is a way of thinking that ensures that no one is left behind, no one is neglected. It is a way of building up slowly, one step at a time, all the while working towards a goal. It is an initiative to align ideas with efforts and efforts with goals. And when it all comes together—whether at work or at home—our lives become richer, our efforts more relevant and our goals more attainable.

5

AADU PULI AATAM[14] AND THE ART OF WORKING TOGETHER

The game of Aadu Puli Aatam
Photo credit: Kreeda

When you next visit a temple or monument, particularly in South India, if you can drag your eyes away from the

---

[14]Also known as Tiger and Goat, *Puli Meka, Adu Huli Ata, Bagh aur Bakri, Bhag Chal*, etc.

breath-taking workmanship and draw your attention to the floor, you could find something interesting.

The floor holds traces of games people have played for decades and even centuries. While in some temples, you could easily find these boards clearly etched on the floor, in some cases, they have eroded over time and can be spotted only with a keen eye and the right lighting. Often, the games are hidden under barricades, construction material and other paraphernalia, sadly obliterating an important clue in our cultural history. The effort taken to search for games and the pleasure of actually finding one is almost akin to a successful treasure hunt.

A short while ago, I visited a large temple and was walking around with my eyes glued to the floor. A helpful passer-by thought I had dropped something and offered to help. When I explained what I was searching for, she got excited and roped in her family to help. Seeing all of us staring intently at the floors, other passers-by offered to help find the object they thought we had lost. Again, I explained my quest and soon there were close to 25 people literally crawling over every inch of the temple trying to locate game boards. Every line and curve and even every flaw in the stone was debated upon as a possible clue to buried treasure. And when a game board was discovered, the cheer and happiness were palpable.

How old are these etchings? No one knows because it is impossible to date an etching. What one does know is that these are etched deep on hard granite floors and, therefore, may not be the work of a stray visitor, as he would lack the special tools. What one does know is that many of these etchings are geometric with straight lines and perfect spacing, and, thus, likely to be the work of a trained craftsman.

Were these games perhaps etched by workmen who were building the temple? Was it their pastime during the afternoon siesta as the sun blazed down? Did the board provide hours of fun in the evenings when the light was too dim to work? A group of people clustered together in the light of an oil lamp, deeply focussed on the game unfolding before them. Or were the stones brought from elsewhere, in later years, to repair damaged temples? No one knows, but it is wonderful to realize that these games that we play today are a legacy of our ancestors.

Sadly, in the name of renovation, many old stones have been removed and substituted with new ones that lack the touch of cultural history. Yet, there is hardly a temple or monument, particularly in Tamil Nadu, where you will walk away without spotting a curious and distinctive triangular-shaped board on the floor. This board was used for the game of *Aadu Puli Aatam* or the tiger and goat game. While there are numerous games to be found, this is by far the most prevalent in the state.

These etchings give us ample proof of the popularity of this game because one can often find multiple boards of this game, all within a distance of a few feet of each other. Was it sheer popularity? Did numerous boards near each other reflect some kind of competition space? The questions are numerous, but sadly we may never get the answers. What we do know is that there are numerous boards to be found, with some artisans adding frills and embellishments to personalize their boards. In one temple,

there is actually a signature at the bottom of the board—
an enterprising player claiming ownership and therefore
priority of use! How little life has changed from those days
to the present-day schoolboy, who writes his name on a
cricket bat so he can play first and control its use!

An etching of the game with the signature of the player at the Yeri Katha
Ramar Temple in Chennai
Photo credit: Kreeda

The game of Aadu Puli Aatam is played in numerous
variations across India and parts of Southeast Asia. Among
the more popular ones are *Hat Diviyan Keliya* or *Demala
Diviyan Keliya* from Sri Lanka or *Bagh-Chal* from Nepal or
Bagh aur Bakri in many parts of our country. In India, the
game is known by numerous names and has variations in
terms of the shape and form of the board and the number
of counters or game pieces used. The game boards vary
from the popular triangular board bisected by parallel lines
and the circular ones that are divided by a symmetric

cross to square ones of varying sizes and combinations.

Another version of the Tiger and Goat game from Kapaleeswarar Temple in Mylapore, Chennai. This photo was taken in 2009. Sadly, due to renovations of the temple this board can no longer be seen
Photo credit: Kreeda

Hunt Games

From a simpler game of one tiger and three goats to more complex ones played with varying numbers of goats and tigers, the game has been a source of fun and interaction for years. Perhaps the most popular and widespread of the versions is the one found across South India, played using three tigers and 15 goats.

However, no matter what the variations, the essence of the game stays the same. These games and its variations are classified as 'hunt games.' In such games, one player's pieces are 'hunting' those of the other. The first player tries to capture and kill the second player's pieces, while the second player tries to avoid getting captured by surrounding or blocking the hunter.

What makes these games distinctive is the unequal size of the opposing forces. The hunter usually has fewer game pieces, while the second player or the hunted has a larger number of game pieces.

Interestingly, there is another family of hunt games known as Tafl games—of Nordic and Celtic origin—played on a chequered game board with two armies of uneven numbers. Evidence of archaeological discoveries of Hnefatafl games and the pieces used are found in various Viking burial sites attesting to the games' popularity going back as far as the fourth century.[15] Hnefatafl games are still played in Europe, with championships being organized.

Did these two families of hunt games develop simultaneously or was there a point of commonality? Did travellers, traders or mercenary soldiers carry the games across the world? Did they play the game over an evening with locals around a campfire during their travels? Did they carry the memories back home and imbue it with their own culture, so it developed into a completely different game? No one knows for sure. But the fact remains that hunt games have been around for centuries and there is enough evidence in India to believe that these games have been played by our forefathers for generations and carry with them the wisdom of the ages.

---

[15]Wu, Katherine J., 'This Glass Gaming Piece May Hail from First Viking Raids in England', *Smithsonian Magazine*, 10 February 2020, https://bit.ly/3jAIZvG. Accessed on 13 April 2022.

How Do You Play?

This is a game played by two people or two teams. One player is the goat (defender) and the other, the tiger (challenger). In the most popular version of the game, the challenger has three tigers, while the defender has 15 goats. The challenger has to kill five goats, while the defender tries to surround the three tigers in such a way that the challenger cannot make a move.

The game begins with the two players taking turns to place their game pieces on the board. After three turns, when all the pieces representing the tiger have been placed on the board, the tiger is free to move. The player representing the goat must wait till all 15 game pieces representing goats have been placed on the board.

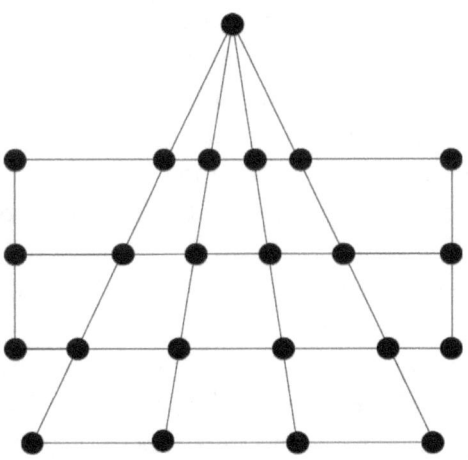

Illustration of Aadu Puli Aatam
Illustration credit: Kreeda

The movement of the pieces should be along the lines and one place at a time. Cutting or killing a goat can be done by jumping over it to land on an empty space behind. Multiple jumps are not allowed, nor is it permitted to jump over two game pieces at a time.

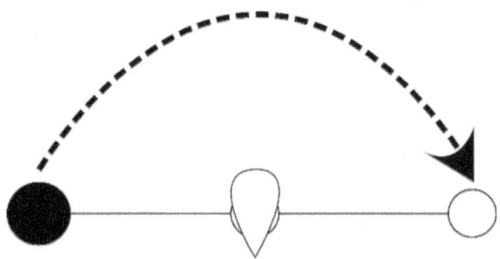

Illustration showing the tiger jumping over the goat
Illustration credit: Kreeda

As the tiger can move first, it is imperative for the player representing the goats to place the game pieces with care. The game involves concentration, skill and strategic thinking.

So, let us examine why Aadu Puli Aatam is considered a hunt game and not just a strategy game like chess. The key aspect that distinguishes hunt games from others is that they are asymmetrical. The two sides neither have the same number of game pieces and moves, nor the same aims. And yet, they are equally balanced.

In this game, one player has three tigers and the other 15 goats. The aim of the tiger is to kill the goats and the aim of the goats to surround the tigers so they cannot move. The tigers kill by jumping over a goat, while a goat cannot jump at all. So, what we have is different aims, different number of game pieces and different types of moves.

Take chess as a contrast, where both opponents have the exact number of game pieces and the exact aim, which is to capture the opponent's king. While different pieces may have different moves, each piece a player has is mirrored by an equivalent piece of the opponent.

In many ways, a hunt game is more akin to real life because you seldom meet an opposition that is identical to you. Whether at work or in everyday life, opposition comes in various forms and sizes—some seemingly innocuous like the goats, others terrifying at first glance like the tiger. And if games are a metaphor for life, understanding the opposition, who is so unlike us in every way, and overcoming the same is a challenge we have to face.

Coming Together as a Team or Community

But perhaps the greatest lesson we can derive from this game is that there is strength in numbers, and when a team works together looking out for one another, there is a greater possibility of success. Many of us have grown up with stories of teamwork. The story of how pigeons trapped under a net worked together to lift the net and escape has perhaps been in every school textbook at one time or the other.

However, the lessons in Aadu Puli Aatam is not just as simple as a homogenous group working together towards a common goal. It is not merely sufficient to work towards a goal, it is about ensuring the safety, security and well-being of the entire team; of looking out for one another and protecting each other, and bringing together the ideas and differences of a heterogeneous group of people.

Having played the game of Aadu Puli Aatam numerous times, I have learned that the person playing the goat cannot afford to sacrifice a single goat without weakening their position.

This is again in contrast to chess, where game pieces are regularly sacrificed to strengthen a position or acquire an advantage. Clearly, the idea is about how the good of all is greater than the good of the individual. This concept of common good goes back to the early Greek philosophers.

Aristotle was clear that there is greater value in the common good than in the individual good, noting in his *Nicomachean Ethics* that '...even if the end is the same for a single man and for a state, that of the state seems at all events something greater and more complete; ... though it is worthwhile to attain the end merely for one man, it is finer and more godlike to attain it for a nation or for city-states.'[16]

Interestingly, the game of chess is a game of kings and zamindars. This was almost a training for battle and strategic thinking. Numerous chess boards made in marble, jade and even silver, speak of this royal legacy. Essentially, this reflects the priority for a ruler or leader: the common good.

On the other hand, Aadu Puli Aatam is a peasant game. It was drawn on the ground with a stick or on the floor of a home with a piece of chalk. Seeds, stones or even broken twigs were used as game pieces. Unlike chess, where you can sacrifice a piece to attain a stronger position, you can never do that in Aadu Puli Aatam. The minute you sacrifice a piece, you weaken yourself. That is the essence of the

---

[16]Aristotle, *Nicomachean Ethics*, Ch. 1.2.

game. This game is for the community and the importance of each and every goat reflects the needs of every individual within the community.

In contrast to common good, individual good is the fulfilment of one's purpose—which is the right and natural thing for humans to do. With these two completely opposing philosophies, one is often puzzled or confused about rights and wrongs. Daniel Callahan in *Individual Good and Common Good in Bioethics* remarks, 'One of the purposes of ethics is to ensure that individual benefits and the common good are in harmony. Individuals do not live in isolation but as a part of a wider society.'[17]

And therein lies the solution, the need for harmony and the working together of leaders and the community. In this case, the community could be the family, society, an organization or even a country. And unless every individual with all their differing ideas, goals, dreams and perspectives are drawn together, it is almost impossible for the community to be strong because every lost individual weakens the community. But if the community is inclusive, non-judgemental and looks out for every individual, then they remain strong.

A few years ago, while consulting with an NGO working with HIV-positive children, I was awestruck by the strength of the community. It was a time when HIV was a relatively new issue, knowledge was sparse and fear ruled the day.

---

[17]Callahan, Daniel, 'Individual Good and Common Good in Bioethics', Monographs of the Víctor Grífols I Lucas Foundation, https://bit.ly/3wogpW2. Accessed on 21 March 2022.

Against this backdrop was the story of two young children, named Benson and Bency (for the sake of anonymity). These children, both HIV-positive, were catapulted into the spotlight in 2003, when they were denied admission to a local school after the parents of other children protested. It took a lengthy public awareness drive, processions by more enlightened members of the community, photo-ops and public appearances by celebrities, who hugged the children to dispel the common apprehensions about the disease. In the end, the children were readmitted to school.[18] This was by no means the end of the issue. It took years of effort before HIV-positive children were allowed to attend school, and even today, there are pockets of issues and discrimination. However, the solidarity of numerous community members in watching out for their own has been critical in the progress that has been made. Much like the game, not a single member of the community can be sacrificed if the community as a whole is to remain strong.

Strategy Can Overcome a Seemingly Stronger Opposition

In this community-led model, we find another brilliant lesson—the seemingly weaker goats can become stronger and seem invincible even when confronted with the menace

---

[18]Philip, Shaju, 'In long, lonely battle against HIV, Benson has lost sister Bency', *The Indian Express*, 7 June 2010, https://bit.ly/3KZnCQb. Accessed on 21 March 2022.

and strength of a tiger. And this becomes possible when the goat plays the perfect strategic game and surround the tiger, thus overcoming the opposition and emerging victorious.

This is much like the proverbial story of David and Goliath from the Bible, where the small and seemingly weaker David, armed with merely a slingshot and five stones, overcame the Philistine giant Goliath, who stood over nine feet tall.

The business world abounds with stories of the underdog taking on the competition. My personal favourite is the story of the Honda Motor Co., Ltd and its foray into the American market. In the 1950s, the American motorcycle market was dominated by one name: Harley-Davidson. Big powerful bikes were iconic in America. However, in a different part of the world, a virtually unknown Japanese company, headed by Soichiro Honda, had been experimenting with small motorcycles since before World War II. He saw an opportunity for a market in America that appealed to a different type of customer than those of the Harleys.

In 1959, Honda opened its first dealership with just three employees. While sales were slow at first, a brilliant advertising campaign with the tag line 'You Meet the Nicest People on a Honda' positioned their motorcycles as fun and economical.[19] Before long, Honda was dominating the motorcycle market. The right strategy and a synergistic plan of product and marketing can often help overcome

---

[19]Drevenstedt, Greg, 'Honda Celebrates 60 Years in America', *Rider*, 8 October 2019, https://bit.ly/3C7x8gV. Accessed on 2 March 2022.

obstacles, even if they are seemingly invincible as tigers or in the case of Honda, Harley-Davidson.

Keeping Your Eye on the Ball

While a perfect game is a theoretical possibility, perfection is not an everyday occurrence. In the hundreds of games I have watched and played, there are numerous times that the goats are playing a seemingly perfect game and yet, one wrong move is all it takes for the goats to weaken their position. In life too, sometimes, one wrong move without thinking of the consequences can have a ripple effect and things can start falling apart. Therein lies another lesson from the game—the need to keep thinking, strategizing and working to pull the community together, so the opposition can be overcome.

This is perhaps best illustrated by an interesting historic inscription found in the city of Chennai. At every point in history, there has been a great focus on the importance of security, law and order, and the ability to survive. An interesting inscription in the Sri Thiyagaraja Swamy Temple in Thiruvottriyur in the north of Chennai gives you a sense of how things worked in the area. Individuals were selected to be watchmen or *kavalkarar* to ensure the safety of the village. For this role, they were rewarded with a tract of land reserved by the villagers for the purpose. Failure to carry out their duty properly was severely dealt with by the villagers. The inscription reads that dacoities had become prevalent due to the negligence of the watchmen, and this in turn was causing them great loss. As many as

48 watchmen were taken to task and punished.[20]

The watchmen were part of the community. By taking their eye off the ball, there was a ripple effect that led to the entire community suffering the losses caused by the dacoities. One fault of the watchmen put the entire community at risk and therein lies the lesson derived from this game—the need to be constantly vigilant and give the opposition no chance to weaken the community. When even one goat falters, or makes a mistake, like the watchmen in the village, all the goats come under risk.

The message of the game of Aadu Puli Aatam has grown more relevant than ever in these times. As communities grow more diverse and viewpoints and ideas change, the need for tolerance, the importance of accepting every member of the community and ensuring their safety and survival is a critical message in the world of today.

---

[20]Raman, K.V., *The Early History of the Madras Region,* 2nd edition, The C.P. Ramaswami Aiyar Foundation, Chennai, 2008, p. 138.

6

DAHDI:[21] WHEN SYNERGY LEADS TO SUCCESS

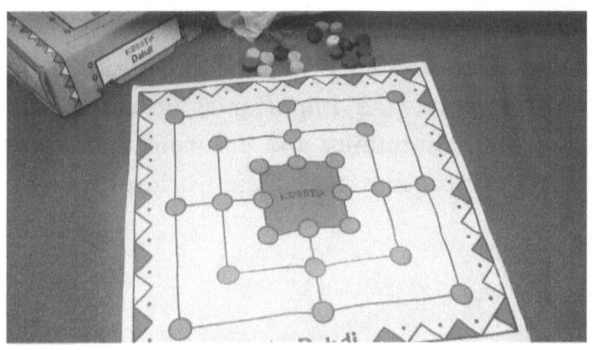

The game of Dahdi
Photo credit: Kreeda

In games, you often come across something that does not quite fit into any classification. You cannot simply label it and call it one type of game or another. This inability to pin it down often leaves us puzzled.

This happens in real life too. We come across situations and people that are difficult to categorize or label. This takes

---

[21]Also known as Nine Men's Morris, *Nav Kakri, Muhle,* etc.

us out of our comfort zone, leading us to think that the situation or the people are not the best for us. But what if we were to look at them differently? We will find that dealing with situations and people we do not understand is precisely what helps us grow as human beings.

Years ago, I had the opportunity to work as a communications consultant with an NGO dealing with HIV/AIDS. While the professional in me was excited by the challenge and the opportunity the project presented, the personal side of me was nervous. Brought up fairly sheltered, my initial interactions with high-risk communities such as transgenders, sex workers and homosexuals left me slightly unnerved. But within a matter of time, I learned to put aside my reservations and interact with them as I would with anyone. I grew to know and respect many of them, and in the course of these interactions, my life changed forever. I became less judgemental—in short, I believe I grew as a person. But it is not just me who benefitted from this. I was able to convert my initial reservations into talking points to be addressed in all communications. Thus, our output was not just informative and effective but answered the very questions, and addressed the very issues that people wanted to talk about and were not able to before due to fear and embarrassment. So, stepping out of the comfort zone was a win-win for all concerned.

Games are no different. Some of them challenge you such that you end up questioning the norms, which in turn encourages you to dig further and come up with strategies and approaches that can address the situation in the game and help hone your thinking skills.

One such game is Dahdi played on a grid of three concentric squares of decreasing size, linked by perpendicular lines.

How Do You Play?

Two players are given nine game pieces each. They take turns placing their game pieces on the board. Game pieces cannot move until they have all been placed. If one player gets three game pieces in a row, he can remove one of the opponents' pieces. Once all the pieces are on the board, the players can move them. Pieces can move only along the lines and cannot jump over another piece. The purpose of the game is to remove seven game pieces from the opponent by getting multiple placements of three-in-a-row.

At the beginning of the game, it is more important to place pieces in versatile locations rather than trying to achieve three-in-a-row immediately. This allows for strategic planning. Dahdi is considered a 'solved game'. These are games whose outcome—win, lose or draw—can be correctly predicted from any position, assuming that both players play perfectly. Since a perfect player is a rarity, this is more of a mathematical exercise.

This is not a traditional three-in-a-row game where the objective is to get three game pieces in a row. Those games conclude once you have three-in-a-row. Here, the objective is to destroy the opposition by removing their game pieces. The multiple placements of three-in-a-row are just the means to an end rather than the end itself. This makes it difficult to classify it as a three-in-a-row alignment game.

But like everything else in life that is different, special games such as these create the best experiences for us. After all, during our lives, the alignments we make, the friendships we build or the network that we need, change from time to time. These are often defined by changing interests, changing lifestyles, changing professions or changing cities. But with every change comes a new set of obstacles or challenges that await us. Our friends or support group, our alignments as they were, are what help us face these situations.

Dynamic Environments

The game of Dahdi precisely reflects these dynamic changes, which are so similar to our lives. When we look around us, we find that in many cases, those who are the most successful are the ones who seek out new alignments or networks. They use these as opportunities to come up with new ideas and stay informed. They are dynamic and driven, but there is always a flip side to it. If these relationships or alignments let them down, they run the risk of losing the advantage. After all, old relationships are likely to be reliable, while new ones are often an unknown factor.

Imagine a game where you are making a plan to create a new three-in-a-row placement and the opposition blocks and prevents you from completing it. The opposition now has the advantage, while you have to rally your resources quickly and try another approach.

In life, there are those who shy away from building new relationships. The fear of leaving the comfort zone overwhelms them and they tend to lean onto a more static approach. Think of a game where a player manages to place his game pieces in such a way that with little effort, he can repeatedly create placements of three-in-a-row. He does not try anything new, but he is comfortable as he is and is still in control of the situation, until of course the opposition destroys the placement. Then the player is left scrambling for a solution.

Like in life, there has to be a fine balance between the cautious approach and the dynamic one. If one can manage that balance with care, then obstacles and challenges could well melt away. The trick lies in learning to balance relationships, continuing to nourish those that have stood the test of time, while seeking out those that could expose you to new ideas, situations and experiences.

Tracing the History of the Game

In a recent archaeological discovery[22], this game board was found etched on stone juxtaposed with Brahmi inscriptions, which are considered one of the earliest-known writing systems in Southeast Asia. While the inscriptions are yet to be deciphered, as some of them are damaged, the word *katta* meaning square, which could well refer to the squares in the game, is inscribed next to it. If this were so, it could help dating the antiquity of the game back to as far as 300 BCE.

However, there is an interesting school of thought that

---

[22]Sauj, M.T., 'Another Tamil Brahmi inscription stone found in a shambles', The *Times of India*, 29 December 2020, https://bit.ly/3xm0o35. Accessed on 13 April 2022.

the inscriptions could refer to a temple plan and not a game. To understand this further, one must understand a little more about traditional temple architecture.

Temple Architecture

While there are numerous acceptable layouts for our temples, one such is described in the shastras as three areas or layers that surround the site reserved for the temple's primary idol which signifies creative energy. In this structure, the outermost layer signifies aspects of asuras and evil, while the inner signifies aspects of devas and goodness. In between the good and evil is the concentric layer signifying human life.

Thus, the plan looks like three concentric squares around a central point. The similarity between this and the game of Dahdi is startling. This could well explain why there are questions on whether the description in the inscription refers to a temple plan or to a game. We will never know till the inscription is translated for us.

Numerous etchings of this game are found in Indian temples and monuments. It is very popular in the Telugu heartland. However, strangely enough, though several boards can be found across the temples in Tamil Nadu, the game seems to have almost disappeared from the memories of people. It is interesting to consider why this happened. Were there changing fashions even in games? Did the game disappear with the waning influence of the Telugu Cholas— an offshoot of the ruling Chola dynasty? One may never know the answer, but it is fascinating to contemplate how history could well influence the popularity of games.

The game of Dahdi from a temple floor
Photo credit: Kreeda

Creating Synergies

The game of Dahdi, with its aim to move game pieces and create alliances on an intricate board such that three pieces align, has deeper significance. This reflects the world, where it is important to create synergies, partnerships and strategies best suited to our needs. In other words, an elaborate three in a row exercise.

Perhaps, the one place where these dynamic synergies have often played a role is the political scenario. Be it the twenty-first century or the ninth century, some things never change. To understand this better, let us look at the political scenario of Tamil Nadu back in the ninth and tenth centuries. Tamil Nadu was primarily ruled by three major dynasties—the Pandyas, the Pallavas and the Cholas. These dynasties were jockeying for power, building alliances and gathering resources to outwit and outflank the others.

In the Battle of Sripurambiyam around AD 879, the Pallavas, under Aparajita Varman (fl. c. 885–903 CE) with the support of an emerging new power, the Cholas, under Aditya I (c. 870/71–c. 907 CE), defeated the Pandyas. But peace and the alliance did not last long. Aditya I, inspired by his success, attacked his ally, and Aparajita Varman was defeated and killed. This battle gave greater power to the Cholas.

Many inscriptions are found in the local temples that speak of the political alliances of the time. In the Sri Thiyagaraja Swamy Temple in Chennai, in what was once a prosperous trading post, there is an inscription about a gift given to the temple by a princess of the Chera Dynasty. Now, the Cheras ruled in Kerala and southern Tamil Nadu. The fact that a Chera princess made a donation to a Chola temple far beyond their political sphere of influence indicates a possible alliance between the Cheras and the Cholas. Other inscriptions speak of the conquests and battles against the Pandyas, and the support they received from the Sinhalese who came to their aid. These dynamic synergies and alignments of power truly reflect the essence of the game of Dahdi, transforming it into a game of networking and political diplomacy.

Interestingly, the game board of Dahdi in the Thiruvottriyur Temple is carved just under the Ekapada Moorthy or the one-legged idol. This unique carving shows

Lord Shiva flanked by Lord Vishnu and Lord Brahma, all standing on one foot—a true divine synergy.

Ekapada Moorthy (one-legged idol) at Thiruvottriyur Temple
Photo credit: Author

The constant and ongoing realignment of game pieces in a variety of combinations to defeat the opponent is symbolic of the ever-changing political synergies of the time.

But synergy is not merely a political exercise or ploy. It is a part of our everyday life. We, as human beings, have to be in constant alignment with our environment. The alignment of game pieces is the alignment of resources, and the synergies we achieve as a result of such alignment determine the outcome. There is no dice in this game and hence no element of chance. The decision is ours. The synergies or alliances are ours to create and the results ours to accept.

Stephen R. Covey, the author of the book, *The 7 Habits of Highly Effective People,* says, 'Synergy is the highest activity of life; it creates new untapped alternatives; it values and exploits the mental, emotional and psychological differences between people.'[23]

In 1988, a young man, following the death of his beloved father, quit his job and returned to his home town. From a young and carefree bachelor, he had to take on the role of the patriarch. His younger brothers and mother looked up to him for running the family business. It was a third-generation business specializing in used cars. It had a brand value, a customer base and a modest profit. It was without doubt a good company, but nowhere even close to the job of his dreams.

After graduating from a top business school, he could not see himself settling down to being merely a glorified used-car salesman. However, at the moment, he had no choice. The family needed him, the business needed him and he had to set aside his dreams.

But this young man was not someone who would let dreams die young. He joined the company and took on the

[23]Covey, Stephen R., *The 7 Habits of Highly Effective People*, Simon & Schuster, 2020.

mantle of running it. Soon, he started to understand the potential in the business—a regular client base who believed in the company, a brand that spanned generations and a domain knowledge that was unique in the city.

Armed with these strengths and a belief in himself, he approached one of the largest international banks that had recently entered the country and was keen to build a large retail presence. His customers often needed loans to buy cars. If he could tie up with the bank to offer loans, he could bring in business for the bank, enable his customers who needed the help and build another division for his business.

It was a synergy and alignment of resources that helped benefit everyone. That was the first step. Soon, the family business came to be known as a one-stop shop for used cars—both buying the cars as well as getting loans for the same. But he was not satisfied. He had bigger dreams.

In a few years, the same young man, who was a few years older and more determined now, approached the bank again. He now had a theory. Anyone who buys a car is perhaps looking for a home—so why not offer home loans too? The bank saw his track record and was satisfied. So, he set up a whole new company. By now the ball was rolling, gathering momentum as it went. Property developers came to know of him and sought his help in identifying potential customers. Before long, he was in demand and able to negotiate with other banks too for distinct loan offers.

With a careful deployment of his resources and effective alignment of market forces and customer needs, he was able to build a flourishing company of his dreams. His interactions with people from different levels brought him recognition and soon he was delivering lectures at the prestigious business school from where he had graduated.

In life, we are in continuous touch with other players in a competitive environment. The same applies for the game of Dahdi. Alignment of three game pieces in a row is similar to the alignment of resources, strategic moves and effective implementation.

Whether it was the Chola king or the young man with a dream, it was the combination of resources, synergies and a tactical approach that enabled them to succeed. But this approach is not just the purview of those in politics or business. It is a necessary aspect of our everyday life.

This philosophy of alliances and synergies, of bringing people together, of capitalizing on the differences between people and of aligning resources is as crucial today as it was in the ninth century. The environment and the political scenarios might have changed, but the elemental human philosophies are the same as they were over a thousand years ago.

7

PALLANGUZHI:[24] THE CUMULATIVE EFFECT OF SMALL ACTIONS

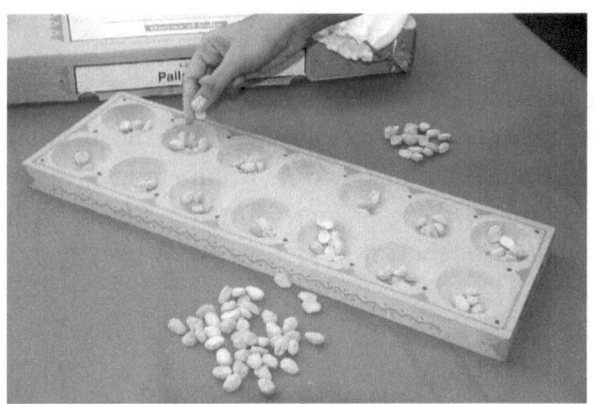

The game of Pallanguzhi
Photo credit: Kreeda

The word 'Pallanguzhi' may seem like a tongue-twister to those not familiar with Tamil. However, it is not a game restricted to Tamil Nadu. Though definitely more popular in

---

[24]Also known as *Vamanaguntalu, Mancala, Olinda Kaluja, Ali Guli Mane, Chenne Mane, Saat Kooti, Kutki-Boia*, etc.

South India, it is a fascinating game of distribution known by many names across the country.

This game is also played in other parts of the world, including Africa and Southeast Asia. It is exceedingly popular across Africa, and even today, coffee shops in many countries there carry such boards for locals to play while they sip on their coffee. It is known across various nations as Mangala, Menkleh, Ayoayo, Awalé, Oware and Wari; in the far East, it is known by names such as Congkak, Dakon, Sungka, etc.

Interestingly, the game has risen to popularity in recent years and games of the type are referred to as Mancala games—a generic name for a family of two-player turn-based strategy board games played with small stones, beans or seeds and rows of holes or pits in the earth, a board or other playing surface. The objective is usually to capture the highest number of pieces through strategic game play.

The name 'Oware' from Ghana, which is one of the most popular versions, apparently derives its name from the phrase 'he/she marries'. This is based on a legend of a man and a woman who loved playing together so much, they decided to get married so they could continue playing together.[25] A true testimonial to an exciting and fascinating game.

Also called pit and pebble games, which is descriptive of the board on which it is played, there are variations across the world as far as the layout of the game, the number

---

[25] Johnson, Alice Otchere, 'How the Ashanti game of Oware was used by slaves in the Caribbean to plan their escape from plantations', Face2Face Africa, 30 July 2018, https://bit.ly/3MtJXai. Accessed on 3 March 2022.

of pebbles, the strategy and the number of players are concerned.

A typical game board has two straight rows of seven pits and optional larger ones for keeping score or storing the captured pieces. In some versions of the game, these larger pits are not limited to storage but also used for distribution of game pieces. There are versions with the board having five pits instead of seven and four rows instead of two. There is also some evidence of a triangular version of the game, but it is hard to determine whether it is an anomaly or a rare version.

In India, the game pieces—typically nuts, seeds, pebbles or cowrie shells—are often defined by the location. Along the coast, cowrie shells tend to be very popular. However, as you move towards the interior, things change. In South India, tamarind seeds are used as game pieces because of their easy availability, as they are an integral part of most recipes. In Kerala, red seeds, often referred to as *manjadi*, is the popular choice. In the North, pebbles were mostly used as game pieces.

There are a number of games played on this board, each with a varying set of rules. However, the essence of the game stays the same—the players drop the game pieces in the pits according to the rules and collect treasure based on the outcome of that distribution.

The rules vary from the simple to the complex, encouraging players to be quick-witted, mentally calculating the odds of scoring a big win. The mathematical ability to ensure success in the game is remarkable.

*A Pallanguzhi board with three optional game pieces; (clockwise from
left: cowrie shells, tamarind seeds and manjadi seeds)*
Photo credit: Author

Although the African version of the game has gained
popularity across the world, the range and complexity
of the games in India is tremendous. Numerous family
heirlooms of beautiful, intricately carved and embellished
boards have kept the game alive in the minds of the people.
Boards may just be pits in the sand made by the heel of
our hand or cut into stone floors or elaborately carved.
They may include a pedestal or be hinged such that they

are folded lengthwise or crosswise to be able to carry game pieces inside.

Just as others, this game too gives rise to the question, 'How did the same game spring up in different parts of the world?' The answer that springs to mind is trade routes.

In fact, during my travels, I was fortunate enough to find two rows of seven pits cut into the floor in an old Roman temple in Palmyra, Syria. The history, the ambience and the very ruins dissolved in my mind with the excitement of finding evidence of what was likely to be a game board. While, of course, one can never be certain, it is likely that this game was played in Palmyra at some point in time. Palmyra was an important stop on the Silk Route for trade between the East and the West in the third century.

I would like to imagine travellers from faraway lands, dressed in exotic clothes and speaking strange languages striking profitable deals, retiring for a afternoon nap and playing a game with new friends from different cultures, sitting in the dim light of oil lamps. It may well be a figment of my imagination, but perhaps it was true and that's how games spread across the world!

The picking up and dropping of game pieces with a single hand might sound simple, but takes some getting used to. Beginners are often found using both hands to drop the game pieces. However, I have witnessed senior players disqualifying a junior one for using both hands. Practise helps and once the rhythm sets in, it becomes easy to understand the calming effect of that rhythmic movement.

Pits cut into the floor of a Roman temple at Palmyra, Syria.
Probably a game of Mancala or Pallanguzhi
Photo credit: Author

The manipulation of the pieces by the fingers is a great exercise that keeps arthritis and stiffness at bay. The handling of seeds, shells or stones in the game is reminiscent of the Greek worry beads. These are often used in therapy and playing the game could well have the same effect. This is also similar to the manipulation of prayer beads worn in different cultures.

One version of the game involves a single player rhythmically distributing the game pieces, with each pit holding a different number of the pieces, ranging from one to seven. Legend has it that in the Sanskrit epic Ramayana, Sita played this game to kill time when she was held captive by Ravana. She made pits in the soft ground with the heel of

her palms and used the seeds of the Ashoka tree.[26] Perhaps
Sita too, stressed by the events of her life, could feel the
calming effect of rhythmically dropping seeds in a pit.

The act of dropping the pieces one by one in the pits
seems to mirror the act of sowing the seeds. So, it is often
called a sowing game. While there are many things to say
about the game, the sheer fascination of playing is what
makes it so appealing.

So How Do We Play?

There are many versions to the game, but let us start with
the simplest one. Five game pieces are placed in each of
the 14 pits on the board. Once the board is set up, a player
starts by picking up the pieces from any pit on his side
of the board and rhythmically dropping them one by one
in subsequent pits, while moving around the board in an
anti-clockwise direction. Starting on his side of the board,
he has to drop game pieces into the pits on both sides.

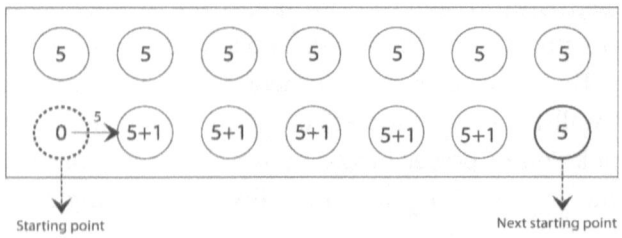

Illustration showing the distribution of game pieces in Pallanguzhi
Illustration credit: Kreeda

---

[26]Vaswani, Anjana, 'Games people played', *Mumbai Mirror*, 3 June 2018, https://bit.ly/3px5uF0. Accessed on 3 March 2022.

Once the player has dropped the game pieces in his hand, he picks up those from the next pit and continues to play. As the player moves around the board, he will encounter a situation where he has dropped the last game piece, but the pit next to it is empty. At that point, he taps the empty pit, moves on to the next pit and collects the game pieces from there and keeps it as his treasure.

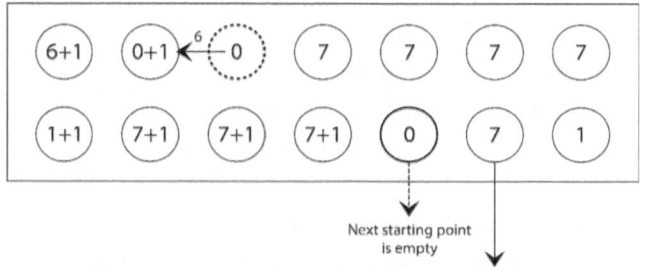

Illustration showing the game pieces in Pallanguzhi as treasure
Illustration credit: Kreeda

He does not drop these but keeps it for himself. It is now the turn of the next player. However, if the first player taps the empty pit and finds the next one empty too, then he collects no treasure. It is still the turn of the next player.

The second player begins on his side of the board and can choose to start from any pit. He then proceeds to play in the exact same manner as the first player. When he reaches an empty pit, he collects his treasure, if any, and then it is the turn of the first player again. It is a turn-based game, and it continues till all the game pieces are collected.

There may come a point in the game when there are a very few game pieces left on the board and playing with them becomes tedious. At that point, players can mutually agree to shut down a part of the board and continue to play on the rest of the board. Sometimes when there are only a couple of game pieces left, players distribute it amongst themselves by mutual agreement. The winner is the one with the most treasure.

In an ideal game, players will continue to play a second round. The person with the least score will contribute his entire treasure. The other player will contribute an equal number. These are distributed five apiece to the pits. Unused pits are shut down for this phase of the game. The game continues as explained above. This can go on for many rounds or until one player is completely wiped out.

While this is the simplest version of the game, there are many more often involving seven, 10 and even 12 game pieces in a pit. In one version, the players get to reserve a corner pit so the treasure that accumulates is theirs for the taking. In another version, a central pit is reserved like a bank where all collections are received, but none can be drawn till the end of the game. These are complex, and for the book, this one version explained above will suffice. However, there is an interesting twist to this version, which is often adopted by the more advanced players. During play, if there are four pieces in any pit on the board, the player on that side can claim it. However, this has to be done immediately after the fourth piece is dropped as the other player can block this move by placing his palm over the pit. This requires the players to be hypervigilant and quick in their responses for once the player has passed over that pit, he can no longer claim the game pieces.

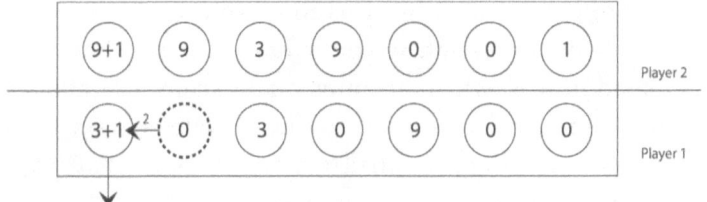

Player 1 has dropped the fourth game piece on his side and can now take these 4 pieces for his treasure collection as a bonus and continue to play

Illustration showing the game pieces in Pallanguzhi as bonus
Illustration credit: Kreeda

At first glance, the game may seem random, and for most junior players, it probably is. However, there was a whole generation who grew up playing this game from childhood and many of them never went to school. They learned how to count by repeatedly playing this game. They honed their skills to the point where they could mentally pick the right move, the right pit to begin distribution. Many of them claim it is simply a mathematical exercise.

I remember my grandmother at 96 playing the game just weeks before she died. She would effortlessly win every single time and grin gleefully at us. Her vision was poor except at very close quarters, but her fingers were nimble and lightning-quick. I asked her over and over to explain how she did it, but she was unable to vocalize any strategy. To her, it was a matter of patterns, numbers and instincts deeply ingrained in her thinking.

Instincts aside, quick wits and quick reflexes often help in playing the game effectively. In everyday life, we are constantly responding to our immediate environment, which is represented by the opponent in the game. Our moves are conditioned by situations we are put in by our immediate environment. We often have to make simple and calculated moves, which at times might seem insignificant, but may impact future success. This game demonstrates the cumulative effect of small actions. It is in that way a miniaturization of real-life situations.

Multiple Small Acts Add up to Success

The concept of the importance of little things is not new to us. We have all grown up with the proverb, 'Little drops of water make the mighty ocean.' Some of us may have studied the poem about how a battle was lost for the want of a horseshoe nail. The Apollo 11 mission could be seen as another example, wherein a circuit breaker was damaged, and all it took was a felt pen to close the circuit and safely bring back the astronauts.

But the game of Pallanguzhi goes beyond merely illustrating the importance of little things like a pebble or a felt pen. It illustrates the cumulative effect of many small actions coming together. This concept is not different from our everyday life.

A young boy was keen to get admission into one of the top colleges in the world. He was rejected by all the colleges on his list the first time he applied. He was depressed, dejected and unsure about what to do next. After many attempts, he managed to pull himself together and decided to apply again.

Sometimes when we fail in our efforts, we tend to give up. But in a game of Pallanguzhi, a poor first round is often compensated in the next. I have seen players lose in the first round, but go on to win the game. And in such instances, we learn some important life lessons. Giving up is not an option. We need to step back, reassess our strategy and try again.

And so, this young man did not rush headlong into the admission process again. He did a careful analysis to understand what was required and where he had failed to deliver. What he understood was that the committee was not looking at one major achievement or goal, but rather at specific aspects of his personality to ensure he was a good fit for the college. It was not enough to have good scores in the entrance exams and ensure good results in his undergraduate course—he needed good internships in his summer holidays, a considerable amount of volunteer work to show his commitment to society, a demonstration of his leadership skills, interest in sports, and most importantly, a good essay that would communicate his potential and purpose. Once he understood that admission was based on a number of small yet significant factors, he planned it better. He waited for two years, slowly building up his resume till he was ready to apply. He was finally accepted into the college of his choice.

We sometimes start focusing on certain aspects of our life so intently that we become oblivious to other things, letting them slip through. There are those of us who neglect our health, our family, our time to rest and recuperate, and it is only later that the impact of the neglect hits us. Much like a game of Pallanguzhi, every aspect of our life, like a pebble, should be properly distributed and seized at the right opportunity to ensure success and happiness.

Today, organizations do not look merely at domain knowledge, but also a person's attitude, aptitude and approach to work. The focus is to look at more holistic individuals who can work as a team. Some even prefer candidates who have a diverse knowledge base, which allows them to adapt to different roles and add to the growth of the organization.

Our pursuit of a goal is not the result of a single act or a single day, but numerous small actions building up over a period of time. The need to constantly revaluate these actions and build up patiently to the final goal is a key lesson. Each aspect on its own may seem small and insignificant, but as parts of a whole, they all matter.

Take the dabbawalas for example. For those who do not know, the dabbawalas work under a lunch box delivery and return system, wherein they deliver hot lunches from homes and restaurants to people at work in India, especially in Mumbai. The dabbawalas pick up the lunch boxes in the morning and deliver them to working people—riding their bicycles and travelling by trains. In the afternoon, they collect the empty boxes and return them to the source. Started in the late nineteenth century, and without the benefit of cell phones or mobile applications, between 175,000 and 200,000 lunch boxes are moved each day by 4,500 to 5,000 dabbawalas.[27] The success of this endeavour was widely

---

[27]Gross, Lotti, 'Forget Uber Eats: Mumbai's 125-year-old food delivery system wins the day', *Adventure.com*, 12 March 2019, https://bit.ly/3vAXU06. Accessed on 3 March 2022.

appreciated and was even quoted in the American broadcast television network, National Broadcasting Company. The article reported that the dabbawalas 'make only one mistake in every six million deliveries'.[28]

The success of the dabbawalas is not the result of one huge effort, but the error-free actions of thousands of people making thousands of deliveries. Each small act adds to the success, much like each pebble in a game of Pallanguzhi.

Based on the configuration of pebbles in the pits, it is up to us to gauge or mathematically calculate where we decide to start. This is done with some understanding of the plausible cascading effect of our choice and actions. But with every pebble that is dropped and every move we make, we need to constantly re-evaluate and calculate those choices. Consciously or subconsciously, we are constantly re-evaluating our moves in life. And if we make the right choices and allow the small steps and decisions to build momentum, then life or our efforts can be successful too, much like a game of Pallanguzhi.

---

[28]'This Indian Food Delivery Service Is the Envy of FedEx', NBC News, 16 July 2014, https://nbcnews.to/3toEsAQ. Accessed on 3 March 2022.

Section 4

....

SURVIVAL

'The most important factor in survival is neither intelligence nor strength but adaptability.'

—Charles Darwin, English naturalist,
biologist and geologist

❖

Sometimes, even the best of intentions or plans or strategies are not enough. Sometimes, it is a fight to simply survive. Life throws us in situations that we need to face and overcome. If we stay true to our goals and balance the choices we make with what life throws at us, all the while adapting to the environment, yet rising above it, we will survive, we will succeed.

8

BAMBARAM:[29] SURVIVING AGAINST ALL ODDS

There is a plethora of traditional games in India. From intricate board games on a variety of fascinating grids that test your intelligence and capacity to think, team games played on open land and fields that require strength and agility like Kho-Kho and games played with tamarind seeds in homes of peasants to games like polo played on horseback, often by royalty, traditional Indian games have enthralled people through centuries.

Many of these, which are dismissed today as children's games, are rooted in religious rites and symbolism dating back to hundreds of years. Some believe that hopscotch or *Paandi*, as it is known in India, had its origin in labyrinths and mazes, and represents the journey of the soul. While symbolism may have influenced many games, for most of us, the fascination is in the sheer joy of play.

---

[29] Also known as lattu, bangaram, pambaram, etc.

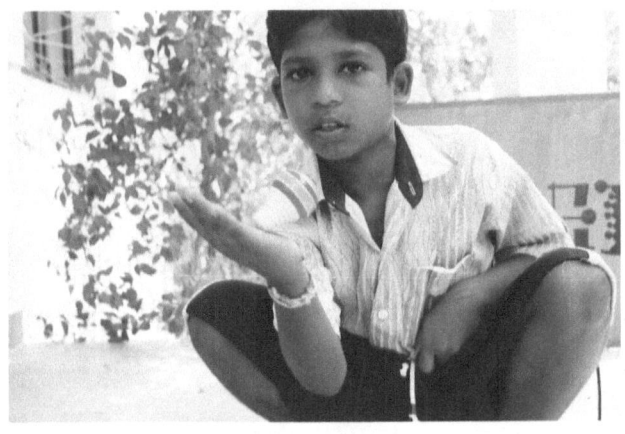

A young boy spinning a bambaram on his palm
Photo credit: Kreeda

While some games are played with everyday material, others are exquisitely crafted. This relationship between traditional games and craft is perhaps rooted in the antiquity of India's craft tradition, which is rich in history and culture, and strongly influenced by the religion, background and attitudes of the rulers of the region. From metalware to textiles, from art and sculpture to woodwork and toys, there are varied and fascinating crafts. One such beautifully crafted game or plaything is the *bambaram* or the top.

It appears that man has always been fascinated with the bambaram—he has the power to spin it and yet defy gravity, given its ability to stand upright on a point, as if magically. It was discovered or invented, almost simultaneously, in several parts of the world.

A bambaram with a wooden tip
Photo credit: Kreeda

There are many varieties of tops all over the world, falling under many classifications. The bambaram is a throwing top. It is generally pear shaped, usually with some sort of pointed end. A cord is wound around the top and when thrown, the cord unwinds causing the top to spin.

These throwing tops are believed to have originated in Asia. A player can hone his skills when it comes to these tops.

The Bambaram as a Scientific Tool

Interestingly, while most games have a close association with religion, beliefs and symbolism, the top has roots in science. In the nineteenth century, scientists and sailors began attempting to use spinning tops as a scientific tool.

The top tends to remain level and upright, even when the point on which it rests is tilted. Scientific tops are called gyroscopes and often compared to the Earth, which is described as a big top turning on its axis.

A gyroscope is a device used for maintaining orientation, angular velocity and is critical in navigation. While spinning, it remains unaffected by the tilting of the surface or mount.

Spinning the Bambaram: Tricks You Can Play

While one end of the rope is wound around the top, the other is held between the fingers. The skill lies in flicking it to the ground such that it lands on the nail or the pointed edge and starts spinning. It requires a great deal of practice to get it right. Once this skill is perfected, many tricks can be played with it.

One of the tricks is to knock out your opponent's top with your own, while it still continues to spin. Another trick is to pick the spinning top up by the string and drop it on your palm while it continues to spin. Some have even perfected the art of flicking the top directly onto the palm, while it continues spinning. My personal favourite was watching a young man 'walk' his top down the stairs. He started spinning it on the top step, then picked it up by the string and dropped it on the next step, still spinning. He continued to pick up the top and drop it on the next step as he walked down the flight of stairs with the top still spinning all the time.

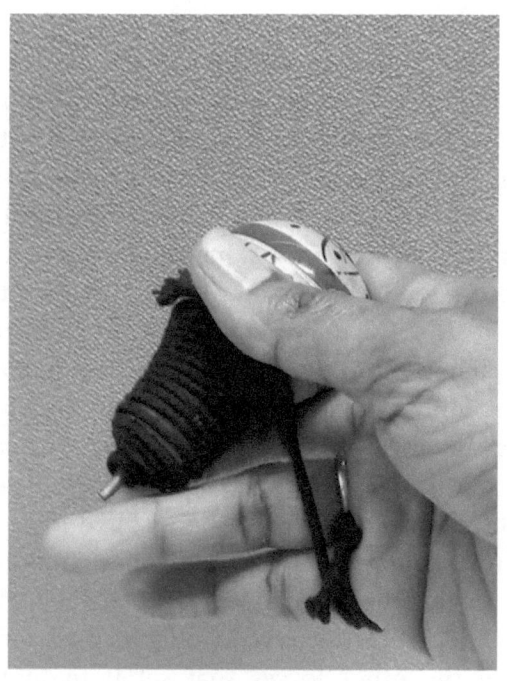

Bambaram with cord wound around it, ready to spin
Photo credit: Author

Lessons from the Bambaram

The basic aim of the game is to pitch and hold the bambaram in its rotating state as long as possible. The game, like any other, reflects the challenges we face in our everyday life. Skills, by themselves, are not enough. Not every well-trained person necessarily succeeds. The purpose of our action needs to be understood. *Yatna* is effort and *prayatna* is well-directed effort.

Pitching is the symbol of understanding and acting with purpose. Whipping the bambaram that produces a sustained high velocity rotation is symbolic of calm thinking and staying power against external challenges. The totality of these skills and attitudes can be summed up as the power of precision and the perfection of delivery. This well-directed human effort is critical in making the bambaram spin.

Interestingly, German writer Franz Kafka wrote a short story called 'The Top' (German: Der Kreisel). In this story, a philosopher tries to grab a spinning top hoping it will continue spinning in his hand. It was his contention that to understand the world he just had to understand one element—in this case, it was the top. However, as expected, the top stopped spinning when he grabbed it.

The top could be viewed as a depiction of the spinning Earth—the populated world that he was trying to understand. Unfortunately, by only focusing on the top, he ignored the other forces that set it in motion—the person and the string.

Handling Distractions

When I started work on this book, I knew what I wanted to write. But life and all that goes with it began to distract my mind. The pandemic, family emergencies, work-related issues—the list was endless. I would make the effort to sit down and write, but would be immediately called away. I started to get frustrated and wondered if I could ever complete this book. It was at that time when it struck me that I could take a lesson from the bamabaram. Prayatna, that takes into account the environment, but still focuses on the core task at hand, was what was required from me.

This happens to most of us. Life takes over and when things do not happen in a certain way or we are unable to do what is required, we get into a cycle of confusion. We end up distracted, working with half-hearted efforts. This results in the symbolic top either not spinning well or not spinning at all. A half-hearted throw results in a half-hearted spin. We need a perfect spin, with the top standing almost still, to be able to call it a success. For this, we need a well-directed throw.

This is echoed in the wise words of Thiruvalluvar, a celebrated Tamil poet and philosopher, who is best known as the author of the *Thirukkural*, a collection of couplets on ethics, political and economic matters and love: 'Plan with a clear brain, and when once you have decided and launched on an undertaking, be firm and unmoved by difficulties and avoid dilatoriness of action.'

Indian literature also refers to putting a top to 'sleep'. This means making a top spin so finely it appears to not move at all!

A person who focuses on his central purpose and is able to work himself to high velocity of action is one who is balanced. He is not only an achiever but also remains calm against external disturbing forces, just like the bamabaram in its apparently motionless state.

Musings on the Lotus

In many ways, the bambaram is reflective of another well-known symbol—the lotus. Though the flower is rooted in mud, it still rises above its murky environment. Based on the unique growing conditions, the lotus symbolizes detachment.

In a similar way, the bambaram, when spun correctly, spins on its point, untouched by the environment. In this lies the lesson that if we are to survive and succeed, we must build the ability to separate ourselves from the environment and focus on what matters.

I am reminded of this boy I have come to know very well. He discovered at a very young age that he was HIV-positive after he lost his parents. Luckily for him, his aunt took him in and cared for him as if he were her own. He knew he could turn to her for love, affection and care. She, in turn, was fiercely protective of him and upset at anyone who ostracized him or mocked him for being HIV-positive.

In spite of growing up in a small town, this young boy has great poise. He is mature, intelligent and speaks well. Yet, there is a certain shyness about him, a gentleness that speaks of a deep understanding of people and life—so rare in someone so young.

He came to meet me with his aunt, who had taken him in, given him a home and supported him his entire life. The boy was completing his BCA and his aunt was proud of him. When they met me, the aunt was angry and narrated how a neighbour had told the boy not to waste his time studying because he was going to die soon.

While the aunt was angry, the boy remained unfazed

by the barrage of insults hurled at him. He took it in his stride. He dismissed the neighbours' remarks, attributing them to their ignorance of the fact that one can live many years with HIV and also to the frustration of their own son not studying enough.

It was wonderful to come across such empathy and understanding. With the encouragement of his aunt and a charitable trust, he went on to complete his MCA, eventually getting a good job with a leading company. Today, the boy is doing remarkably well. Many things helped him—his intelligence and efforts, his aunt's love and care, the financial support he received. However, above all else was his ability to spin like a bambaram, untouched by the words of the neighbour, staying true to his purpose.

Some of you may have heard about or visited the Theopetra Cave in Greece, the oldest known archaeological site in the world, with evidence that humans had lived there 130,000 years ago! While initially believed to be about 50,000 years old, evidence of a child's footprint pushed back Theopetra to over 80,000 years earlier. The site is also home to a 23,000-year-old wall that was most likely built to protect the cave's residents from cold winds.[30]

Just think about it: a footprint that has withstood the ravages of history and the environment for 130,000 years, and a wall that has been a mute spectator to the passage of time.

But that is the power of survival and that is the lesson in this little bambaram—to survive and stand on a point against all odds.

---

[30]Curry, Andrew, 'As Seas Rise, Ancient Footprints Are Revealed', *Sapiens*, 2 August 2018, https://bit.ly/3jG9orH. Accessed on 13 April 2022.

A bambaram spinning on its point
Photo credit: Author

Reinventing Yourself with Every Throw

Many of us may well be familiar with the quote, 'Men may come, and men may go, but I go on forever' from Lord Tennyson's poem, 'The Brook'. While this reflects in some ways the same concept, of a brook untouched by the people who come and go, what distinguishes the bambaram is that it cannot spin forever. Every day brings new experiences and challenges, and it is up to us how we react to these. There are many stories that can inspire us, of people who have risen to the challenges, great or small, and today stand on a point like a bambaram. I believe the best life lessons come from the stories the elderly share with us. It is through their examples and mistakes that we can learn.

In August 2020, a 90-year-old man handed in his hundredth article to a popular fortnightly news magazine. At his age, he could have been easily forgiven for kicking off his shoes and letting life pass by. However, he was unwilling to do so. The article was all the more remarkable because it marked his third choice of career after he retired at the age of 65 as the managing director of a prestigious company. To many, a career starting at the age of 19 and coming to an end with such a senior position would have been sufficient. But that was not the case for him.

He went on to consult with the World Bank for 10 years after that, travelling around the world and advising teams across Africa and Asia. When he turned 75, the World Bank decided he was too old for them and asked him to retire. Instead of retiring, he started helping a small IT firm to grow and build itself. In this capacity, he learned to use the tools of technology. With his guidance and support, systems were established and the company started to grow.

Once the company grew its wings, he realized he had spare time on his hands. He used this opportunity to reinvent himself yet again, and slowly grew to be the special correspondent of a news magazine, meticulously researching articles and meeting deadlines.

Not only did he succeed in every initiative he became a part of, he also changed and adapted like a bambaram that is thrown again and again, and yet successfully goes on spinning.

Even in the world of business, every organization faces such challenges—market forces, legislation, customer feedback, changing financial environment, changes in technology. If organizations do not reinvent themselves to adapt to their environment, their very survival comes under risk.

Leonardo da Vinci is believed to have said, 'Iron rusts from disuse; water loses its purity from stagnation...even so does inaction sap the vigour of the mind.'

Each day brings with it different challenges. Balancing this apparent dichotomy between the dynamic and the static, the changing and the unchanged, the response to the environment and the ability to rise above it is the very nature of human existence and the very essence of survival. It also reflects the nature of the bambaram. When the bambaram seems to stand still on a point, it has not stopped moving, but only gives the appearance of not moving. At that moment, the bambaram is imbued with this very dichotomy of human existence and thus represents every one of us.

To not change and to not adapt is to remain stagnant. Many people mistake stagnation for stability, but they are two different states of being. Stagnation is the bambaram lying unused on its side. Stability is when it is able to stand on its point—truly life's valuable lessons in a bambaram.

9

CHAUPAD:[31] MANAGING CHOICE AND CHANCE FOR SUCCESS

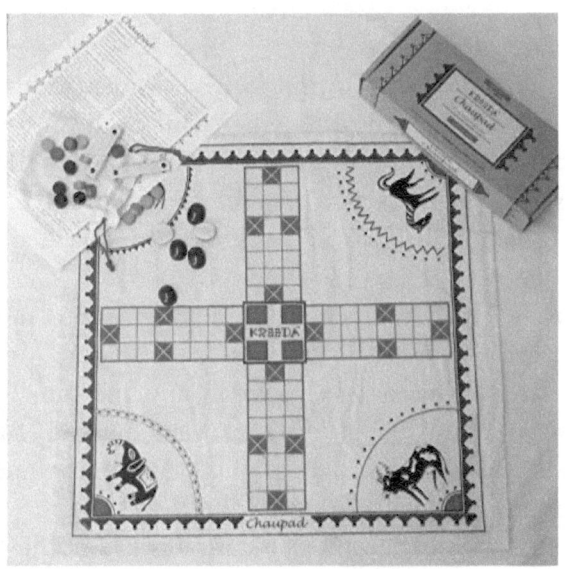

The game of Chaupad
Photo credit: Kreeda

---

[31]Also known as *Pagade, Pachisi, Chaupar, Aksha Kreeda, Dayakattam, Chokkattan,* etc.

Once upon a time, an ardent Hindu devotee called Bhavaji travelled to Tirumala in Tirupathi on a pilgrimage. He was so fascinated by the deity of Lord Balaji in the temple, he decided to stay there forever. In spite of repeated visits to the temple, he could never get enough of the Lord. In fact, his visits aroused the suspicion of the priests, who then prevented him from entering the temple.

Unable to exist without seeing Lord Balaji, he began to pretend that he was spending time with the Lord by playing a game of dice. He would throw the dice and move his pieces and then throw them again imagining that the Lord was playing with him.

One day, the Lord, in the form of a man, actually did visit him and they played together. This went on for many days until something happened. While leaving Bhavaji's room after a night of playing, the Lord left his diamond necklace behind. Bhavaji picked up the necklace and kept it safe, planning to return it the next night.

When the priests opened the temple the next morning, they found the deity missing a diamond necklace. Immediately, an alert was sounded and the hunt for the necklace began. Some of them remembered Bhavaji's frequent visits to the temple and wondered if he had been checking out the place prior to the theft.

Sure enough, when they reached his room, they found the necklace. Bhavaji pleaded innocence, but they would not listen to a single word. When he told them that Lord Balaji had been visiting him every night to play a game of dice, they mocked him.

Finally, he was thrown into a room filled with sugar cane

under the condition that he had to consume all the sugar cane by the next day to prove his innocence. 'Ask Lord Balaji to help you!' they said mockingly and went away.

Sure enough, as an answer to his prayers, an elephant appeared in the locked room and ate up all the sugar cane. As Bhavaji fell on his knees thanking the Lord, the elephant trumpeted. Hearing the sound, the priests came to investigate and were amazed to see an elephant inside the room. Meanwhile, the elephant broke free and ran away.

When questioned, Bhavaji had only one word to say— 'Hathiram'. When asked who that was and how the elephant entered the prison cell, Bhavaji told them that Lord Rama (an incarnation of Lord Balaji) had come to his rescue in the form of an elephant.

Everyone was amazed at his devotion. He was appointed as the head priest of the temple and hailed as Hathiram Bhavaji or Hathiramji.

This fascinating story led me on a quest to find out more in the temple town of Tirupathi. Once there, I tracked down the Hathiramji Math and was shown a shrine with a stylized rendering of a rather corpulent man playing a game of dice with Lord Balaji.

I was amazed. Here was a shrine with a picture of a game similar to the ones I had been researching for years. I stood there mesmerized, thinking of all that had happened to lead me there. As my eyes moved towards the lamp, I saw something more—a cloth game board laid out as an offering to the Lord.

This cloth game was similar to Chaupad. The game of Chaupad played on a board shaped like a symmetrical cross has long been ascribed as the game of the gods in legends and myths. While most people are familiar with the dice game in the Mahabharata and in the tale of Nala and Damayanti, there are numerous stories of the game of dice played by Shiva and Parvati. Most modern renderings of these stories depict the game of Chaupad.

A plaster rendering of Hathiramji and Lord Balaji playing dice
(a wall of the Hathiramji Math)
Photo credit: Author

Now there is no real evidence to indicate this is the game from the myths, but the popularity of the game of Chaupad and its versions across the country cannot be disputed.

So How Do You Play?

The game is played on a board shaped like a symmetrical cross with eight squares arranged in rows of three along each of the four arms. It is a two-to four-player game with four game pieces assigned to each. A player starts on his side of the board and his game pieces travel up and down the arms moving along the board in a clockwise direction till they return to the home side. Then the game pieces travel along the middle line of the arm to reach the safety of the large central square.

An embroidered Chaupad board
Photo credit: Author

Interestingly, the Aztec game of Patolli bears a number of similarities to the game of Chaupad. Patoli is believed to carry a heavy focus on gambling. The story goes that there was a time when Spanish priests forbade people from playing the game during the Spanish conquest of Mexico, presumably because they were selling themselves and their families into slavery over it. It is believed that those who were caught playing Patolli had their hands burned as a punishment!

Some versions of Chaupad have arms that are only six squares long, and in South India, some of the boards have a corner square where one arm joins the other. Versions differ in rules and in throw pieces, with some using long dice and others using cowries.

A version of the game with six squares
inscribed on the floor of a house
Photo credit: Author

The purpose of the game is to take the game pieces safely around the board and bring them home to the large central square. If the opponent cuts a game piece by landing on it, that piece has to start again. The crossed squares are safe squares and a place to stop and take a breather when dealing with the opponent.

There is a twist. Players can move their game pieces in pairs. A pair can only move with an even throw of the dice and half the number of spaces. So, if the throw is six, the pair can move three places and if the throw is four, the pair can move two places. There is another twist—a pair can only be cut by another pair. Interestingly, this rule has now been adopted by Ludo. However, 30 to 40 years earlier, it did not exist.

Another twist that adds further excitement to the game is that a game piece that has reached the safety of the central square can choose to come out again as a 'ghost.' No rules apply to this game piece now. It moves in the anti-clockwise direction, can kill a pair, can kill on safe squares and can spread mayhem. This piece can only be stopped by another 'ghost.' The havoc played by such piece in a game is very akin to a large-scale disaster where all rules are flouted. We witness such situations in life, where nothing is safe anymore, nothing is sacred and nothing can be controlled— earthquakes, tsunamis, riots, war and pandemic. These have the capacity to turn our lives upside down.

It is easy to dismiss this game as merely a dice game, or a game of chance, but the fact remains that the player controls numerous aspects of the game. He chooses which game piece is to be moved, when to cut an opponent's game piece, whether to move in pairs, when to break up the pairs, whether to return as a 'ghost'—many details like these define the outcome of the game.

When the dice is thrown, it creates a few possible ways and constraints within which specific moves can be made. These are similar to our immediate environment, which, at any given time, gives us a fixed number of resources that can be employed in different ways to maximize long-term advantage. Thus, the game becomes an interweaving of choice and chance, much like life itself.

Destiny and Karma

When it comes to destiny and karma, there are various points of view. The most prevalent one is that there is no destiny. Man is free to take all decisions and has to bear complete responsibility for every decision. He alone is responsible for every success or failure. While this is perhaps true in numerous situations, certain things are beyond our control. This could be as overwhelming as a natural disaster or a pandemic, or even as simple as a flat tyre. Another theory believes that our actions regulate the direction of our life and our future. However, we have no control over the outcome.

In daily language, 'destiny' and 'fate' are synonymous, but with regard to nineteenth-century philosophy, the words gained inherently different meanings. Fate is about the present, where every decision an individual has made has led them to the present scenario. However, destiny is the future scenario, which cannot be determined only by decisions an individual will make.

The fact remains that life is a fine balance between choice and chance. We have the ability to exercise our free will in numerous aspects of our life, much like a game of Chaupad. However, the element of chance, of forces beyond our control, the impact of other people's actions even, much like the throw of a dice, will have an impact on the outcome or success of our efforts. Interestingly, this idea of representing God's will or chance in a game of dice is present in many cultures and many references.

Albert Einstein is believed to have remarked, 'God does not play dice with the Universe.' Einstein, of course, believed in mathematical laws of nature, so his idea of a God was someone who formulated the laws and then left the universe alone to evolve according to these laws. In more contemporary and popular culture, the pop group ABBA in their song 'Winner Takes it All' says:

The Gods may throw a dice
Their minds as cold as ice
And someone way down here
Loses someone dear...

Closer to home, Shiva and Parvati are often pictured playing a game of dice. Don Handelman and David Shulman, in their book *God Inside Out: Siva's Game of Dice*, actually ascribe the existence of life itself to a game of dice. Their theory is based on the numerous quarrels that ensue between Shiva and Parvati over the game.

Before the game, the godhead is androgynous, an amalgam of male and female elements—already sufficiently separated to be identified as such yet fused together in a holistic mode. They quarrel, and their conflict rapidly degenerates to the point of breakdown, until the game itself is abandoned, imploded from within. This rupture then leads to even more radical forms of separation. If the androgyne enters the dice game, he/she is torn apart, ripping open the gap between genders and alienating one from the other. Indeed, it is important for our existence that she win... If the goddess wins, that means creation; if Siva wins, that means the opposite of creation. In other words, if Parvati wins, lower levels of the cosmos, including our own, externalize and come into existence.[32]

Whether or not the game of Chaupad is responsible for the creation of life, it is without doubt a fascinating game with important life lessons for us. Let us examine some of the moves in the game and what we can infer from them.

The Throw of the Dice

Every throw of the dice creates certain possibilities. Rather than treating the dice as an alien element that forces us to function under certain conditions, the possibilities that open up should be emphasized. In 2020, the pandemic resulted in lockdowns across the world. While it led to large-scale loss of life and livelihood, it also encouraged many people

---

[32]Handelman, Don and David Shulman, '*God Inside Out: Siva's Game of Dice*', Oxford University Press, 1997, p. 24, 27, 75, 85.

to explore other possibilities. Talk shows and workshops went online, making them available to more people across the world rather than restricting them to a single geographic area. Many people who worked from home found the opportunity to read more, experiment with new hobbies and spend more time with their families. While it may be difficult to look at the pandemic as a positive force, the fact remains that there is an opportunity in everything—to change, to grow and to explore new ideas.

The throw of the dice opens up numerous possibilities. Which game piece do I move? Do I chase down and attack an opponent or focus on getting myself home safely? Am I playing a defensive game or an attacking game? Am I going to carefully manoeuvre my game pieces from one safe square to the next or am I going to take a few risks in the hope that it will pay off? Am I going to have all my game pieces on the board or am I going to play them one at a time? Do I spread my resources or take a more focused approach? Am I going to move my game pieces in pairs and sacrifice speed in the interest of safety? Am I going to focus more on winning my game or in preventing the opponent from winning his game? If a game piece reaches home safely, am I to bring it out again as a ghost to cover and support the other pieces or do I feel more secure with at least one safe game piece?

Every throw of the dice brings up these questions belying the belief that this is merely a game of chance. The questions are numerous. The options are numerous. The choice is in our hands. Life is like that. Many situations and possibilities open up in our life. Some may be the result of chance...

the throw of an imaginary dice. The decisions are still ours to make.

Many years ago, I met a customer who wanted to buy traditional games from me. We got talking and I happened to mention that I was a communications professional too. Interestingly, he was looking for a communications consultant for an international NGO working in the field of HIV. I was not looking for a project and wasn't even sure if I wanted it. But chance brought it into my life. I agonized over the decision for days, wondering if I wanted to find the time, wondering if I would enjoy the project, wondering if I could deliver. Finally, I made my choice and took up the offer. Little did I know that the interplay of choice and chance was to take me on a journey that would change my life forever.

But not every decision we take has earth-shattering consequences or a catastrophic impact on our lives. Some of them are as simple as choosing to wake up in the morning, choosing the clothes we wear, choosing to go to work or skip it, choosing a movie to watch, choosing what to eat or read, and even choosing to read this book!

Some studies estimate that an average human being makes 35,000 choices a day.[33] That is truly a mind-boggling number. While most of the choices are perhaps instinctive, many are made with an understanding of the situation. The fact remains that even if gods play dice, a number of choices

---

[33]Hoomans, Dr Joel, '35,000 Decisions: The Great Choices of Strategic Leaders', *Leading Edge*, 20 March 2015, https://bit.ly/3twYngY. Accessed on 3 March 2022.

are within our control and many of them have the capacity to change the course and quality of our lives.

John C. Maxwell, an American author who has written numerous books on leadership, put it perfectly when he said, 'Life is a matter of choices, and every choice you make makes you.'

Imagine a game of Chaupad. You are sitting with your friends and all of you start with four game pieces each. The goal is the same: to ensure your game pieces reach the central square. You can picture the fun and laughter—the cries of delight on cutting an opponent or escaping to a safe square, the groans when you get cut. The game is alive with fun and interest, whether you win or lose.

Now imagine the same game played without dice. Every move is yours to choose. No dice defines how far you can move. On your first turn, you can pick up a game piece and move it all around the board and safely enter the central square. Can you imagine that game? Where is the fun? The excitement? The exhilaration that comes with success? That special ingredient that adds the essence to the game is no other than the element of chance generated by the dice.

Life has often been compared to a game. And it is this interplay of choice and chance that lends it its essence. What we need to do to survive is to understand it, learn to take decisions based on our knowledge and our instincts, learn different approaches to different situations and then hold on to our seats, for the game of life can be as thrilling and exciting as a game of Chaupad.

10

GILLI DANDA:[34] THE ART OF SETTING GOALS

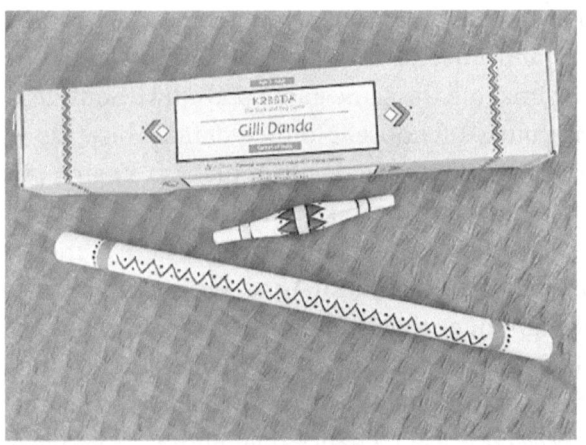

Gilli Danda
Photo credit: Kreeda

In the Hindu epic Mahabharata, the Kauravas and Pandavas often used to play games together, and one such was the game of vita. It was a game in which a finger-size wooden

---

[34]Also known as *Kuttiyum Kolum, Ilatha Kittipul, Iti-Dakar*, etc.

piece is hit over a distance by a long stick. The story goes that the vita hit by the boys fell into a well and they stood around wondering how to retrieve it. At that time, Drona, the would-be teacher to the boys in military science, was passing by. Seeing the situation, Drona, the expert marksman that he was, shot arrow upon arrow such that the vita could be pierced and extracted from the well. This, at the same time, became a lesson in marksmanship for the young princes.

The game of vita, also called Gilli Danda, is one of the most popular outdoor folk sports believed to have originated in the Indian subcontinent. A longer stick is used to tap a short peg of wood tapered or sharpened on both ends so that it can be 'tipped up' into the air and then struck while it is airborne. Games of this type are played in many countries across the world.

There are several interesting versions of this game. In some parts of Kerala, a stump (as in cricket) is placed near the playing pit. The player hits the small stick placed in the pit. From where it falls, the opponent has to throw the small stick towards the player at the stump. If the player hits it, he wins. If he does not, he plays again. If the stick hits the stump, he is out.

With sticks available aplenty, it was easy for children and adults alike to hand whittle them. However, this led to problems. The sharp edges of the stick, when hit uncontrollably, caused serious injuries, often hurting the eyes. This led to a decline in the popularity of the game, especially in urban areas, as open spaces became premium. Sadly, the skill of tapping the gilli and striking it while it is up in the air is slowly becoming obsolete.

It has become necessary to change the image of the game and examine its safety aspects. By ensuring availability of rounded smoother edges, carefully crafted by artisans, the eyes can be protected. Under controlled circumstances and in open spaces, Gilli Danda can still be a wonderful game to play and a great skill to learn.

Today, the game is often dismissed as a game for country bumpkins and a rural sport. Noted Hindi writer Munshi Premchand wrote a short story titled 'Gulli Danda'. The story revolved around two friends from youth. While the first was very poor at the game, the second excelled at it. As they grew up, the first friend went away to the city and returned many years later as a government officer. The second friend stayed where he was and became poorer and poorer. When the friends met up again, the first friend challenged the second to a game of Gilli Danda in the mistaken opinion that his success would mark his victory in the game. He won the game partly through deceit and partly through the indulgence of his friend and continued to believe that success in his professional life had touched all aspects of his life. While watching a local tournament the next day, he realized that his friend was still excellent in the sport and was merely indulging him.

To revive this ancient sport would not only help the preservation of our culture, but would help developing hand–eye coordination and skills that come with the constant practising of the game.

Rules of Play

The game has numerous variations, some of which are similar to bat and ball games, like cricket or baseball. The winner is the person or the team that has scored the highest points. If the player is hitting first, he has to ensure that his performance cannot be exceeded by subsequent players. If he is playing second, he has to outperform the earlier player. Either way, there is pressure on the performer—the pressure of having to outdo the unknown competition or of setting performance standards.

High performance under pressure and against the unknown are typical of numerous situations in life. A student applying to college has to ensure his application is better than other students in order to be accepted into the course and institution of his choice. Previous history of admissions may be indicative of the set standards, but ultimately each application cycle is uncertain and unknown.

A young graduate applying for a job has to have a resume that impresses the recruiter. He has to perform better in the interview than any other candidate in order to be considered for the job. Unlike a board game where the opponent is before you and their moves are visible, giving you some indication of the capacity, ability and tactics, the opponent in Gilli Danda forms an unknown factor. You might have seen him play before, but your basis for assessment is only history. So, a weak player could have a surprisingly good day and upset a stronger player. Every player has to be prepared for every eventuality and perform at his optimum—an interesting lesson on always giving your best. Simple games hold profound lessons only if we have the capacity to perceive them.

In most cases, the game is played by two teams of six players each. The distance hit by each player is measured in terms of the long stick and points awarded to the player. The one with the higher score wins. Though there are numerous rules of playing the game, we will focus on the simplest of all.

How Do You Play?

The first player estimates how far he will hit the gilli. Success is based on estimating correctly, and hitting the gilli neither under, nor over the estimated distance. This exercise in setting the goal is an interesting aspect, unique to this game. The creativity of our ancestors in devising unique games from simple materials is simply astounding.

After setting the goal, the player taps either of the two tapering ends of the gilli, so it hops up in the air, and he hits it as long a distance as possible. If he misses the gilli, he is out. If he hits the gilli, it can be just a single hit or multiple times while it is airborne. The latter requires skill and timing, and helps the player earn bonus points.

Once the gilli is hit and lands, the distance is estimated. The opponent either accepts the estimate and concedes the points or challenges it, in which case the distance is measured. If the distance hit is below the estimate, the player is out. If it is above, he gets points but only for his estimate. If the estimate is right, the player gets his points and a bonus for being right and then plays again. This procedure is repeated until all players are out. Then the second team plays its innings.

Goal Setting

The focus in the game is on how participants set their goals in order to maximize what they perceive as their objective. Our attitude towards setting goals is one of the most critical aspects of our life. We are forever setting goals or deadlines.

'Will complete a project by the weekend...'

'Will read two books a week...'

'Will exercise four times a week...'

'Will take time off every year to rewind...'

In the workplace, setting goals could get more intense. A sales team has to estimate their targets for a year, quarter and even a month. Team leaders have to assess the performance capacity of every member.

An IT company involved in the corporate sale of software products had two sales teams, each focusing on a different range of products. Every year, the team leads were expected to provide the management with their projected targets for the upcoming year. Incentives were based on these targets, and, therefore, became a tense exercise. Over the years, the team leads faced different scenarios.

One team leader tended to be very cautious, always setting low targets and greatly overachieving on the numbers. She had the satisfaction of reaching the target every year, but frustration started to build, as incentives were based on set targets and not on what was actually achieved. Had the target been higher and had her team achieved the same, the incentive received would have been higher too. The other team leader was anxious to get a higher incentive and, therefore, set very high targets. The team fell short and was unable to achieve their incentives.

Estimating high and falling short is a waste of resources, and also demoralizes the team. The leader, who chooses a high estimate unrelated to the capacity of his team, is a high-risk taker with a higher chance of failure.

Estimating low and performing high is sometimes not practical in real life. There should be enough resources available for an unexpected and unplanned high performance. In the example above, financial plans were not made for the unexpected high performance and so incentives were only for the set target.

Thus, the team leaders learned from their experiences and changed their targets the next year. The first team leader made a mistake. One of the products her team was selling was going through a major restructuring. She failed to take this into account. The upheaval in the market due to the change resulted in her being unable to achieve her target. Meanwhile, the other team lead faced two resignations and had to hire new people. She did not invest time in training, and, therefore, she too fell short of her target.

Any target or estimate needs to be set with the full knowledge of the circumstances. In the game, the team leader must know the capacity of each person in the team and anything else that is likely to impact their performance. In real life too, we need to understand every aspect before setting our targets. We also need to plan for the unexpected.

High performance capacity (hitting for a longer distance), tenacity (not getting out) and the ability of the leader to estimate team capacity, assess his resources and determine a challenging but realistic goal are aspects that are put to test by this game.

Many aspects emerge when we play this game. What kind of person is the player in this scenario—a person who prefers to play safe and is averse to risk or someone who is willing to take a chance, take a risk so as to win big or someone who just gambles without taking the needed calculated decision?

Another aspect that emerges is how much effort a player takes to understand the scenario before setting a goal or a target. Do they do their homework? Do they understand the circumstances, the environment and the factors that influence the performance? Have they used the knowledge to the best of their ability?

Often in life, we set goals without understanding ground reality. A little boy who dreams of flying to the moon can be excused as he is a child. But as we grow up, it is often easy to confuse dreams with goals. A dream is something we hope to achieve, but is rarely rooted in reality or in the nitty-gritty of everyday world. It is rooted in hope and desire, not in facts and understanding. Goals, on the other hand, are rooted in understanding the ground reality of what is required to achieve it.

In Gilli Danda, some people often play a second innings. This second chance has its own insights for us. It is a chance to correct the mistakes of the earlier innings, a chance to modify our thinking based on the happenings of the first innings. This chance at course correction to rectify or rethink also takes place in life. A professor I knew used to say, 'Don't make the same mistakes again. It is a sign that you are not learning. If you must make mistakes, make new ones.'

The resulting estimates and scores for the second innings based on the experience of the first one could be revealing. The variations in choices, estimates and their effect on scores could be indicative of how much the team has learned from the past.

The focus is not on the team that scores higher, but on the one that gets closer to its estimate. And if both are equally close, then which one is higher in terms of score. A team that is within 90 per cent and 110 per cent of the estimate might be the better performer with reference to the knowledge of its capacity. Although the team outside this range may have a higher score, it did not know itself well and therefore did not estimate its capacity properly.

It would be wise to remember that estimates in the second innings cannot be based only on the performance in the first innings. In games, as in life, other aspects change—the environment, the wind perhaps, a player injury or fatigue. These too must be considered before setting the goal.

Why Set Goals?

An important aspect of setting goals is to understand why we set goals. To continue the game analogy, what are the factors that influence the team leaders in making their estimate? What do they hope to achieve? Is it to win, to maximize the score, to try and achieve what no one else has, the thrill of the risk or the satisfaction of achievement or simply to have fun? So many things contribute to our goals, each with a different reason, a different purpose.

What matters is not just setting the goals, but understanding the risks that come with each goal. A young man I knew was fortunate enough to get his dream job within a few months of graduating college. Not only was it the job of his dreams, but it was in a location of his dreams and with an organization of his dreams. These things do not happen very often, and needless to say, he was excited and happy with the job. There was just one fly in the ointment. The salary was not as high as he would have liked it to be. However, he was clear in his mind that the salary did not matter as much as his job, his role and the company itself. In his mind, he had reached his goals. With his clarity towards his goals, he was able to avoid frustration.

We set goals almost every other day. While some are critical and require deep thinking and planning, some are simply based on estimates. One way or the other, the need to set goals and estimates, the need to understand the rationale behind them and the need to be able to achieve them are critical aspects of life. They are also the essence of the game of Gilli Danda.

Section 5

....

THE WORLD AND YOU

'Everyone thinks of changing the world,
but no one thinks of changing himself.'

—Leo Tolstoy
Russian author and Nobel laureate

❖

As trite as it sounds, life is a journey with ups and downs and often it is us, our responses to situations, our ability to handle them and our efforts to learn from them that define the moments of our life. We can never control everything...not the environment, not the world at large, but we can learn to control what we do, what we say and what we think in every situation. While the throw of the dice takes us to situations beyond our control, it is within us to use those situations to learn, grow and change ourselves, for when we change ourselves, we change the world.

11

PARAMA PADAM SOPANAM:[35] THE INTERPLAY OF VICES AND VIRTUES

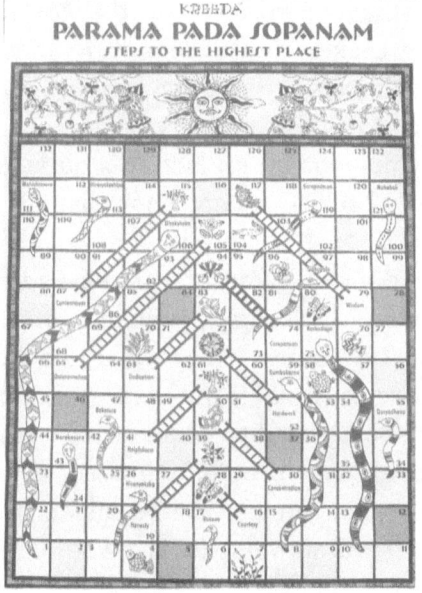

A version of Parama Padam Sopanam
Photo credit: Kreeda

---

[35]Also known as Moksha Patam, *Vaikunta Pali, Gyan Chaupad, Gyan Baazi,* etc.

No book on traditional games would be complete without the game of Parama Padam Sopanam or Snakes and Ladders. This game has travelled to the West and come back to us in a simplified avatar; it has won the hearts of millions of children all over the world.

While most of us have grown up with the game and are familiar with the modern board that has 100 squares, the traditional boards have varying grids with a varying number of squares. A version of the game played by Jains even has grids that are not quite rectangular, but designed to represent the *lok purusha* or the cosmic man. The positioning of snakes and ladders also varies from board to board, but almost each of them has one large snake that takes you back to almost the very beginning or sometimes even the very first square. In fact, it is quite likely that the English phrase 'back to square one' was coined from this very game.

In the traditional game of Parama Padam Sopanam, traces of Indian philosophy, thinking and culture are explicitly found in almost every square of the board. The top of the board generally features the devas or gods, while the rest of the board used to be peppered with illustrations of birds, animals and people; and then, of course, there were the snakes and ladders. While ladders are an obvious symbol of upward movement, the use of snakes needs greater understanding.

In Hindu philosophy, the symbolism of snakes is complex. Vishnu is usually pictured lying on Adishesha, the mighty serpent. Hindus worship snakes in temples as well as in their natural habitat, offering them milk, incense and prayers. Vasuki, the Serpent King, played a vital role in the churning of the ocean.

But coupled with this worship is a deep fear of the snake. With India being home to four of the most poisonous snakes in the world,[36] Indian people respect snakes. It is perhaps this aspect of the snake, the fact that it can bring a human being down by just a bite, that has made it the central symbol of this game. Metaphorically, the snakes represent vices.

Game pieces typically start from the square numbered one and move through each square on the board, based on the throw of the dice. The movement of the game pieces has been described as a boustrophedon (ox-plough) track. The word 'boustrophedon' is a style of writing in which the starting point of alternate lines of script is reversed. This contrasts with our standard styles of writing in which lines always begin on the same side, usually the left, in most languages. The term comes from ancient Greek meaning 'as an ox turns while ploughing'.

If the throw of the dice takes a game piece to the base of a ladder, then the player climbs up. However, if it takes the game piece to the head of the snake, the player moves down. The player who reaches the last square first is the winner. It is a simple race game based on sheer luck and so cannot produce experiences that can be extrapolated to real-life situations.

The essence of the game comes from elsewhere. In this game, every snake is named after Indian mythological

---

[36]K. Mukherjee, Ashis, 'The "Big Four" Snakes of India', Springer Nature, Singapore, 2021.

characters whose vices or flaws ultimately led to their destruction. The ladders, on the other hand, represent virtues or the path of dharma that will take you through life and enable you to reach the highest place or moksha.

Different boards have different names for the snakes. However, I have come across some obscure boards, the names of which are not familiar. Could they perhaps be names of characters from local communities representing vices? While we will never be sure, this is possible, as numerous local versions of games existed at the time. Since they were printed on paper, many have disappeared completely.

The basic essence of the game is clear. The player acquires virtues and moves up through life to reach parama padam or moksha. If the player acquires vices, he plunges downward pushing moksha further and further away.

However, there is more to the game than just that. To understand this, we need to understand some basic aspects of Hindu philosophy. In Hinduism, the concept of *purusartha* or the object of human pursuit refers to the four aims of human life—dharma, artha, kama and moksha (righteousness, prosperity, pleasure and liberation).

While all of them are considered important, dharma gets precedence and directly leads to moksha. It is interesting to note the sheer practicality of Hindu philosophy: it gives space to both prosperity and pleasure, which form a large part of our life. Rather than frowning upon this, it accepts the two, rooting them all in dharma. I am no expert, but I found this truly fascinating. Perhaps this is why our festivals, too, are a fusion of rituals and merrymaking.

The other face of the coin is the *arishadvarga* or the six enemies of the mind, which are *kama, krodha, lobha, mada, moha* and *matsarya* (lust, anger, greed, arrogance, delusion and jealousy). These are the vices or flaws that could prevent a person from following the path of dharma.

In Hindu theology, without experiencing the consequences of the arishadvargas, a person cannot fully evolve and understand the need for dharma and divinity. It is not about preventing or avoiding the vices and flaws, but accepting them and achieving mastery over them—that is critical to the growth of a person.

The other aspect that I find fascinating is the belief that as a person's awareness increases and as he appreciates the power these flaws hold over him, he begins the journey to moksha. The mere power of his *sankalpa* is good enough. Sankalpa means an intention or resolve to focus on a goal or change an aspect of one's life. This determination to improve or change is illustrated in numerous myths of demons and villains begging for forgiveness after they are defeated. Narakasura, a demon who was defeated by Krishna, begged for forgiveness and requested that all celebrate his death with colourful lights. Today, the festival of Diwali is associated with Narakasura in some regions.

When we look at this in the context of the game, it becomes even more fascinating. The snakes represent arishadvargas, the ladders the purushartha, with dharma leading directly to moksha.

In real life too, with or without the religious overtones, we realize that in the long run, virtues help us advance, succeed, and find peace and happiness, while vices hold us back or hurt us personally or the people around us, which in turn affects our sense of happiness.

This can be best illustrated by the stories behind the characters represented by snakes in the game. Lovers of literature will know that Aristotle described hamartia or the fatal flaw in a character that leads to their downfall.

Shakespeare's celebrated tragedies encapsulate this very aspect. From the jealousy of Othello, who murdered his wife based on a rumour, Lady Macbeth, whose greed and ambition encouraged her husband to kill the king, to Hamlet's anger and desire for revenge, the fatal flaw ultimately results in their downfall.

Closer to home, let us look at the story of Mahabali, which features in numerous boards. Legend has it that Mahabali was a good king and much loved by his people. Unfortunately, the love of his people and the prosperity of the kingdom made him believe that there was none like him on earth or heaven. His pride was his undoing. The gods decided to teach him a lesson. Vishnu took the form of a short, young priest and visited Mahabali during a puja. Mahabali rashly promised him anything he wanted. The young priest requested three paces of land. Mahabali was scornful of such a small request as he believed he had it in his power to give the priest so much more than what his small feet could cover in three measly steps. But the boy would not take anything else, so Mahabali granted him his wish. Suddenly, the young priest started to grow in form; he kept growing until two of his giant footsteps covered the earth and heavens. There was no place for the third footstep. Mahabali, realizing his sin of pride, bowed and offered his head for the third step. His pride led to his undoing; his fatal flaw caused his downfall. Interestingly, his acceptance of his arrogance lead to forgiveness and his stature as a good and just king who comes back from the netherworld to visit his people is celebrated every year through the festival of Onam.

This sense of grey pervades much of the game. Human beings and even those demons represented by the snakes are not seen as good and evil, but rather inherently flawed. It is the flaw that needs to be addressed, needs to be brought under control in order to progress on the path to moksha. And if one can accept it in all humility, focus on overcoming it, then the path remains open.

We all struggle with our flaws, but if we allow them to rule our lives, we lose the ability to grow. The flaws do not make us demons, but human. It is the ability or the strength to overcome them that is needed.

In most boards, there is one long snake, Dhakshaka, representing anger. The story of Dhakshaka is one of how uncontrolled anger can lead to destruction. One day, King Parikshit, the Kuru ruler, was hunting in the forest and got lost. He found himself near a hermitage and sought the help of a rishi. The rishi, however, was in deep meditation and did not respond. The angry king draped a dead snake around the rishi to show his frustration. Meanwhile, the rishi's son, who had been away, returned. Seeing what had happened, he cursed Parikshit to be killed within seven days by Dhakshaka, the snake prince. The king took every precaution, but the curse could not be undone. Dhakshaka took the form of a worm and hid himself in a fruit. When

Parikshit bit into the fruit, the worm transformed itself into a snake and killed him.

This destructive power of anger is something we witness in our lives. The anger that causes us to break, to kill, to injure another is corrosive, destructive, and, as indicated by the size of that snake in the game, more powerful than any other vice. As the problems in our environment increase, as our frustrations grow greater, anger takes over, destroying everything.

The traditional game of Parama Padam Sopanam or Moksha Pattam is a metaphor for life itself. With virtues and vices interwoven into the very fabric of the game, along with fables and myths, it becomes our journey to reinvent ourselves in every step of the way as a response to the environment and the world in which we live.

ACKNOWLEDGEMENTS

The journey towards understanding more about the relevance of traditional games began many years ago during conversations with Mr N.S. Parthasarathy, my father. Together we explored all the games and what meaning they could perhaps have today, in various facets of our life. Until then, my research and efforts were focused only on understanding the rules of traditional games and reviving them.

When the idea of this book was conceived, I always believed my father would be a part of this journey. Sadly, that was not meant to be. So, I must first acknowledge and thank my father for helping me discover this aspect of traditional games.

I would like to thank my parents for the upbringing I had. I was not curtailed in my thinking or vision. It didn't matter if something had never been done. We were encouraged to try it and that confidence helped me greatly on this journey of discovery.

I would like to thank my wonderful husband, who has supported me through all my mad ideas. They exhausted him, bemused him, but he was nevertheless unwavering in his support!

I would like to take a minute to remember my grandparents, who brought such joy to my children.

The children revelled in the pampering of their great-grandparents. Without those special interactions over traditional stories and games, my interest in this subject may never have come into being.

I would like to make special mention of two people who have encouraged me, pushed me and believed in me through the writing of this book.

Pradeep Chakravarthy, with whom I spent hours discussing various aspects of games and who has used many of my games in his training programmes, read and critiqued some of the chapters and helped me dig deep and do better.

T.T. Srinath, who, along with his wife, has always encouraged me to do more, and believed in me long before I believed in myself. His lovely wife Lakshmi and I worked on a project designing saris based on traditional games, one of the most wonderful projects I have done, and I cherish those saris to this day.

If I were to name every person who helped me on this journey, the list would be longer than this book. But there are some people of whom I must make special mention: my friends Vidya Chandar, Susan Thomas, Sunandini Pattu, Susan Das, Radhika Muthukrishnan, Priya Krishnan, Sanjay Rao, Ashwin of Odyssey, M.Ct.P. Chidambaram, Govind Iyer, Gita Ram, Nandita and many more have helped me, encouraged me and have been sounding boards for this book and other aspects of my life. Their confidence in me and their encouragement has always made it easier to do things.

I would love to list all those who have supported me by playing my games, by sending me photographs of games in temples where they've been; people who have aided my research and participated with such joy at every event; and my team at work—the list is endless. So, all I can do, is say thank you, for I am fortunate to have such a wonderful support system.

I would like to specially thank Mr Mehra of Rupa Publications, a wonderful man, who reminds me so much of my father. The idea of the book came over a conversation with him, and through all the ups and downs that followed that conversation, he encouraged me to complete this.

The team at Rupa—Kapish, Yamini, Sandhya, Sakschi and everyone else were a joy to work with, and I thank them for their support and efforts in bringing out this book. I would like to thank Ms Jaya Jaitly, Mr Harsha Bhogle and Mr Arvind Swami for readily agreeing to do the foreword and endorsements for this book.

Thank you so much for helping make this dream come true.